D1328359

REDFIELD PROCTOR

PROCTOR

The Story of a
Marble Town

BY

DAVID C. GALE

1922

THE VERMONT PRINTING COMPANY

Brattleboro, Vermont

TO

REDFIELD PROCTOR

PIONEER

WHOSE PERSONALITY

IS STILL A VITAL FORCE

IN THE COMMUNITY

IN WHICH HE LIVED

THIS LITTLE BOOK

IS RESPECTFULLY

DEDICATED

FOREWORD

THIS book represents the work of many different people. The most that the writer has attempted to do is to take what others have been kind enough to give him and fit the pieces together, like the parts of a picture-puzzle, each in its proper place. The result, as the title implies, is a story rather than a history. It lacks the completeness of a reference book. Its chief virtue is that it is short, and that though it masquerades under the name of story—it is, according to the best of records and traditions, a truthful account of the town's growth. If it helps the reader to see the wonder and the romance of that growth, it has accomplished all that anyone could ask of it.

In the spirit of fairness, as well as of gratitude, acknowledgment is hereby given to Mr. Harry P. Powers and Mr. Frank B. Kingsbury, who began the work of collecting material; to Mr. Frank C. Partridge, Mr. B. F. Taylor, Miss Emily D. Proctor, Mr. Hamilton Ormsbee, Rev. Frederick W. Raymond and Rev. William H. Cassidy, who have contributed generously to the text; to Mr. Redfield Proctor and Mr. Mortimer Proctor, without whose support the project would have been long ago abandoned; and to Mr. James T. Glasson, for his resourcefulness in providing photographs.

A word of appreciation is due also to the long list of older residents who have submitted without protest to what must have seemed like an endless chain of questions. It was left with them to turn back the years, so that others might get a glimpse of the days that are gone.

D. C. G.

7

CONTENTS

LIST OF ILLUSTRATIONS

11

LOOKING SOUTH FROM THE MARBLE BRIDGE

CHAPTER I

MARKING THE TRAIL

NO one knows when the Indians lighted their first camp fire in the Otter Creek Valley. As far back as 1609 when Samuel Champlain turned the prow of his boat toward the shores of Vermont, the land on every side was in possession of the Redskins. It is supposed that even then they were old in the work of planting corn and carrying on tribal wars.

In Crockett's History of Vermont it is maintained that "for nearly eighty years the Coughnawaga Indians, a tribe of Iroquois descent, on various occasions sought to establish a claim to a large area of land in Vermont based on the Iroquois occupation. Their claims made to the Vermont Legislature were to the effect that their hunting grounds in the state were included in these bounds:

"Beginning on the east side of Ticonderoga, from thence to the Great Falls on Otter Creek (Sutherland Falls), continuing the same course to the height of land that divides the streams between Lake Champlain and Connecticut River, thence along the height of land opposite the Missisquoi, and thence to the bay."

The legislature contended that the treaty between France and Great Britain in 1763, and between the United States and Great Britain in 1783, extinguished all Indian claims to Vermont territory, and declined to vote money to the claimants.

Prior to 1730, if we may trust the completeness of the records, the Otter Creek had never been traversed by a white man. On April 27th of that year, a small band of Indians, captained by James Cross, set out from what was then known as Fort Dunmore in Massachusetts and blazed a course northward toward the waters of Lake Champlain. They traveled by way of Black River, Plymouth Ponds and Cold River. On Sunday evening, the third day of May, they camped on the banks of the Otter Creek. The following day they built canoes, and by Wednesday they were afloat on the lonely picturesque stream that was even then beginning to weave itself into the history of the Green Mountain State.

The diary of James Cross contains this entry:

"We go in our canoes upon Arthur (Otter) Creek till we meet two great falls in said river (Gookins Falls and Sutherland Falls). Said river is very black and deep and surrounded by good land to the extremity of our prospect. This day's travail—35 miles."

The Otter Creek, in those days of Indian trading, was the natural thoroughfare between Canada and Massachusetts. Prices were lower in the States and the goods thus acquired were pushed up through the Otter and Lake Champlain and delivered to the buyers of the North Country. Although this system of merchandising was continued without interruption until the outbreak of the French and Indian wars, there is nothing to prove that any white man passed over the course between the years 1730 and 1748.

In May of the latter year, the Melvin Expedition was formed. The leader was Eleazer Melvin and there were eighteen men in his party. Starting from Fort Dunmore on May 13th, they proceeded up the Connecticut to Charlestown, where they swung off to the Black River, taking a trail that was practically identical with the one over which the Cross pioneers had tramped. It is to Melvin's diary that later generations are indebted for those thrilling observations which have already been retold in Mason's History of Rutland County:

"On the 19th the party crossed several large streams, being branches of the Otter Creek. Saw many signs of the enemy, such as camps, trees girded, etc. On the 20th marched over Otter Creek around Sutherland Falls. Further along found several camps of the previous winter and beaten paths made by the enemy. On the 24th came upon a camp fenced in with a very thick fence where was found a keg of about four gallons which appeared to be newly emptied of wine and about twelve pounds of good French bread. Reached Lake Champlain on the 28th and had a skirmish with a party of Indians. Began a retreat, pursued by about one hundred and fifty of the enemy. Came again to the banks of the Otter Creek in Pittsford, about a mile below Sutherland Falls and marched to Center Rutland and made camp. Thence followed up the Otter Creek to the head of one of its branches. Had another skirmish with the enemy which scattered the party; four of our men killed, one wounded and one taken prisoner."

It was only a few years after Melvin's scouting party, that the cry arose for something better than a trail across the wilds of Vermont; France and England were each claiming the same territory and were having no end of trouble over the settlement. It was often necessary to send troops into Canada but the Green

Mountain region was a handicap that no one liked to consider. Soldiers had to pick their way by the marked trees along the path. Supplies must be packed upon the backs of horses, a method which was extremely hazardous under the conditions that were then menacing the country.

Throughout all that region, there were only two or three settlements. A little group of men had made a stand at Dummer's Meadow on the Connecticut River. Block houses had also been reared at certain other points farther north, including the French Canadian camp at Chimney Point on the lake front. In the main, however, there was little else than untouched forest, in the conquest of which lay untold danger and hardship.

In 1756 Massachusetts began to agitate the subject of a military road between the Connecticut River and Lake Champlain. The Legislature went so far as to call for a survey which should indicate the perplexities of the undertaking. It was planned to lay out the road from Charlestown on the Connecticut to that point on Lake Champlain which was in line with Crown Point, N. Y. Since the survey was to be staked by way of Otter Creek, there was demand for facts and figures relative to the depth of the water, the number and size of the falls, and the character of the soil and woodland along its borders. The survey soon became a reality but it was three years before the road began to grow.

In 1759 General Amherst gave the order which was to bring light to the forest-burdened hills and valleys. He directed that some of the New Hampshire and Massachusetts soldiers, stationed at Crown Point, should be drafted into the service of road-building,

and so it happened that 200 men under the leadership
of Capt. John Stark marched out from the Fort, armed
with shovels and axes, and attacked the unlimited
leagues of woodland. As they fought their way on
toward the Otter, they left behind them a wagon
track in place of the trail. At the end of that year the
road had crept to the banks of the river. A bridle
path was extended over the mountain by Colonel
Hawks but for some reason he left his task uncom-
pleted. In 1760 the New Hampshire soldiers went
to work at Number Four and stretched forth a new
road as far as Ludlow, the point where Colonel Hawk's
path terminated. From that time on, there was far
less uncertainty in the transporting of supplies over
the Green Mountains. Military stores could be hauled
on wagons to Ludlow and then on the backs of horses
up over the heights to the shores of the Otter Creek,
where they were transferred once more and pressed on
toward the lake.

It is not within our province to review all the hor-
rors and bloodshed of the Colonial and Indian Wars.
All readers of history know how, by reason of its situation, the Vermont territory was harassed by the raids
and outrages which usually fall on the neutral ground.
There could be no serious thought of settlement when
the element of safety was entirely lacking. Many of
the New England pioneers had passed through the
great forest and marvelled at its possibilities but few
had cared to undertake the risk. Civilization was
confined to the military posts and blockhouses.

The turning point came in 1760 with the British
victory on the plains of Abraham. It was inevitable
that the surrender of Canada and the march of General
Amherst to take possession of Montreal in the name of

VILLAGE OF PROCTOR IN 1922

the English sovereign should set people to thinking about the friendly land to the southward where nature was standing ready to open the doors of her storehouse. Then began the crusade for town charters directed against the amiable Benning Wentworth, Colonial Governor of New Hampshire. Nearly all the towns in Rutland County were chartered in 1761 although in many instances there was a space of several years between the granting of the charter and the first settlement. There was really no incentive for hurrying since the annual dues on each charter were limited to a single ear of Indian corn for which the trustees of the town were to be held accountable.

"In the spring of 1766," as the story appears in Crockett's History, "John Chipman of Salisbury, Conn., with fifteen other young men set out for the new lands of the New Hampshire Grants, taking oxen and a cart laden with farming tools and other necessary articles. They found no house north of Manchester, and probably no road beyond Sutherland Falls, where the village of Proctor is now located. In some places it was necessary for this pioneer band to cut a path. The party followed the valley of the Battenkill to the head waters of the Otter Creek, and at Sutherland Falls a canoe was fashioned from a large tree. The ox-cart was fastened to the stern of the canoe and was towed up stream, while the oxen were driven along the bank. In this manner the young men proceeded to the present site of Vergennes, where the waterfall interrupted further navigation."

In the midst of all this land distribution, Lieutenant-Governor Colden of New York issued a momentous proclamation. The document quoted from a late order of the king which named the Connecticut

River as the boundary line between New York and
New Hampshire and it cautioned the pioneers against
disobeying that order. From a previous title granted
to the Duke of York the boundary had been described
as a twenty mile line extending northward from the
Hudson River to Lake Champlain, and up to that
time the Vermont lands had always been recognized
as a part of the New Hampshire province. It was on
the strength of this older edict that Governor Wentworth had apportioned the Vermont townships.

No sooner had Colden sent forth his decree than
he, too, began to issue land patents in what is now
known as Rutland County. His proclamation was
penned in April, 1765, and by the following November
he had meted out about twelve hundred acres. These
were supposed to be awarded in return for military
service but they were usually turned to the profit of
the land speculators. Few of them had the king's
approval.

Then was ushered in one of the most sensational
struggles that this or any country has ever recorded.
Out of it arose Ethan Allen and his intrepid Green
Mountain Boys, a body of men which the New Yorkers
were never able to conquer. It was due largely to the
Allen leadership that Vermont finally won the contest
and the right to enter the Union as an independent
state. The holders of the New Hampshire grants had
undergone untold dangers and privation in the rearing
of their rude cabins in the wilderness and they resented
any action which might endanger their houses and
lands. They adopted a form of resistance that left
no doubt as to their intentions. More than one land
interloper was sent back across the lakes bearing on
his back the unmistakable marks of the persuasive
"beech seal."

In the staging of this exciting drama, the scenes were often unrolled in Rutland County. The Otter Creek Valley, even at that time was looked upon as a land of promise, and the Rutland section, in addition to its wealth of untouched soil had several alluring mill sites, each of which might be made to produce its tribute of lumber and corn meal. Furthermore, the Valley at this point had a natural beauty and charm of setting that one would hardly expect to duplicate throughout the entire length of the river. On every hand was a glorious vision.

Only a few years ago, a man who has traveled much, both in this country and in other corners of the world, confessed to a fellow tourist that he had found nothing to equal the view which flashed upon him as the train emerged from the rock-hewn cut at Sutherland Falls and bore him out among the tantalizing lights and shadows of the colorful Pittsford valley. This is an opinion of the present. If the picture is worthy of such a tribute today it must have been even more worthy of it in those long ago days when the entire landscape was set forth in the rare harmony which nature alone can arrange.

What then was this "Great Falls" country which the Indians knew? Uncurbed woodland for one thing— beech, birch, maple and spruce on the higher levels, and pine and elm bordering the rivers and lakes—a stretch of forest in which the deer and the bear, the wolf and the otter were seldom disturbed by the bark of a gun. Underneath the trees was a soil that needed only to be turned over to bring forth all that the pioneer could desire. On all sides, save at the peak of the highest mountains, was the rich drapery of a perfect vegetation, cut in twain in the lower valley by the sinuous, gleaming course of the Otter.

Among the soldiers who took part in the French and Indian Wars there was at least one who was unable to forget the captivating charm of the Pittsford valley. Others might admire and pass on but with Gideon Cooley the impression was of another kind. And so in 1766, he journeyed back again up the old military road until he stood once more on the height which overlooks the Great Falls. From that vantage point he attempted to pick out the site for a new log cabin. His eye finally settled on a tract of land that bordered the river on the east and thrust its corner up under the very nose of the falls. The beavers had already built a home at one end of it, causing the water to settle back and overspread its surface but he planned to open the dam and develop the fertile acres.

After giving the tract a closer inspection and finding his confidence unaltered, he began to look about for the man who controlled the title. The owner, one Captain Doolittle, having in mind the settlement of the town, was ready to grant him the deed on condition that he settle on the land and bring it under cultivation. Under those conditions Cooley signed the paper and went back again to Greenwich, Conn., his former home, to prepare for his conquest of the wild.

In the summer of 1767, Gideon Cooley, in company with his brother Benjamin, made still another trip up the Crown Point Road to the land at the foot of the Falls. Once there, they began clearing away the timber and in the course of time they raised a cabin in the open space. So far as is known, this cabin was the first to be reared within sound of Sutherland Falls. The land on which it stood was later incorporated in the town of Pittsford. Nearly all the original Cooley land is now in Pittsford, although it is conceded that the little corner which jutted up under the falls may have come within the present boundaries of Proctor. The chronicles of those early days cast only a meagre light on the lives of the Cooley brothers. Nor is it essential that we should know how they tamed the forest and wrested a living from the stumpy soil. It is enough to know that they had the fortitude and persistence to hold them here until others arrived with aid and companionship. There is little danger of over-estimating their fighting spirit. On the one hand were the redmen and the four-footed foes; on the other, were the undrained swamps, charged with disease and death. Courage these men must have had in unstinted measure, otherwise they could never have kept their heads above ground.

SUTHERLAND FALLS QUARRY, 1885

CHAPTER II

THE COMING OF SUTHERLAND AND OTHER PIONEERS

FIRST HOUSE AT THE FALLS—THE SUTHERLAND MILLS—
SOCIALBORO LAND CONTROVERSIES—SUTHERLAND
AND HIS NEIGHBORS—THE REVOLUTIONARY
PERIOD AND THE MAKING
OF THE STATE

W HEN Cooley drove his first stake in the wilderness, he thought only of the land and of the home he proposed to build. His plan contemplated the clearing away of the trees and the tilling of the soil; to him the river was simply a thing that must be forded. But not all the prospectors who passed that way were inclined to look upon the river as an obstacle. Hardly had the Cooley brothers started their work in the valley when there came a man who believed he could divert the power of the falls to his own enrichment. That man was John Sutherland.

The date of Sutherland's coming has never been definitely fixed although it is fairly certain that it was not later than 1767. What we do know is that he took up his claim at the Falls under a New York charter in what was then designated as the town of Socialboro.

A number of New York land traders had applied to the governor of New York, John Henry Lydens, for a new town. It was to comprise all of the present towns

27

of Rutland and Pittsford and a part of Brandon. Sutherland was one of the men whose names appear on this petition and a likeness of the governor's original charter is even now one of the treasured legacies of a certain Clarendon family.

The mere fact that Sutherland was intimate with the British officers at Whitehall was enough to bring him trouble. When in 1771 William Cockburn, a surveyor and a friend of Sutherland, was sent down by the New York governor to survey the Socialboro acres, he was met by James Mead and Asa Johnson, the self-appointed delegates of the Hampshire Grant settlers. After these gentlemen had outlined to Cockburn what would happen if he continued his operations he gathered up his instruments and retreated to more hospitable territory on the other side of the lake.

In a letter to James Duane of Albany he described his experiences as follows: "I was not allowed to go to Sutherland's house, although I had run out lots from the south bounds to within two miles of the Great Falls where he lives. I found it in vain to persist any longer as they were resolved at any event to stop us."

When it became known that Sutherland was in sympathy with Cockburn and the interests which were back of him the former was promptly cast under the ban of suspicion. Nor was he able to reinstate himself in the confidence of his neighbors. There is little doubt that in the course of time he thought it best to buy the New Hampshire title to his land, thus winning from the Green Mountain Boys a reluctant acknowledgment of ownership, but even that was not sufficient to raise him from the probation into which he had fallen. The Socialboro settlers were so ardent in their adherence to the Vermont cause that any deviation to another standard was viewed with reproach and condemnation. The ancestors of John Sutherland came to this country from Scotland and made their first home at Horseneck, Conn. From there they moved to Nine Partners, Dutchess County, N. Y., and it was from this latter settlement that the Sutherland family made its entry into the wooded basin of the Otter Creek. The house which they reared at the Falls, a cabin of exceedingly modest size, must have been a marvelously elastic structure, otherwise they could never have packed into it the thirteen children which made up the household. It is hard to believe that it was ever recognized as a tavern even though there is a tradition to that effect. On the other hand perhaps it was not altogether a disadvantage to have it snugly packed, for at best those first winters in the wilderness with only the fireplace to drive out the frost must have been a serious tax on the endurance.

The Sutherland home stood two or three rods west of the river and a little southwest of the marble bridge of today. The shingles were put on with wooden pegs, and so were the roof-boards. The sides were first filled with mud and later plastered. It was never painted. It was torn down by M. C. Warner in 1872. The site is now marked by the Myron Warner house. In fact the position of the two structures was so nearly the same that the first cellar was utilized in part as a foundation for the second building. It would seem that Sutherland must have raised some sort of cabin for a temporary shelter, since tradition has it that the timber for his house came from his own mill. There is reason to believe also that the grist mill was the first to be constructed, so there must have been a roof to cover the Sutherland family while all this was going on.

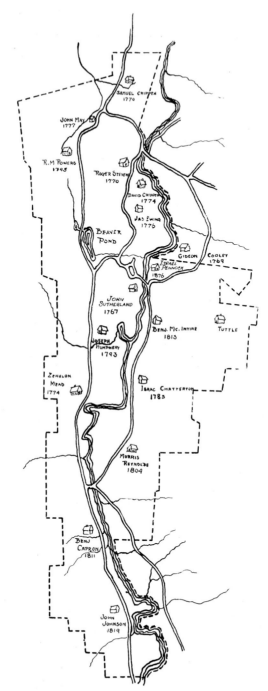

MAP SHOWING APPROXIMATE POSITION OF THE FIRST SETTLEMENTS
IN WHAT IS NOW THE TOWN OF PROCTOR

The ground on which the early saw mill rested is now covered by the south-east corner of the Vermont Marble Company's Electric Shop and the grist mill was a little farther up the course of the river. Both were very near the falls. It is said that the sawed lumber could be slid over the rocks to the pond below, where it was made into rafts and floated down stream to the waiting buyers. There are actual entries in the Pittsford records which prove that lumber was being produced by Sutherland in 1780. Old authorities claim that Fort Vengeance was built of Sutherland's lumber.

The grist mill also was patronized very generally by the pioneers. They came from all directions traveling mostly by paths or trails.

There is a wood road on West Mountain which follows the line of the old bridle path past the set of farm buildings at the summit. Over this trail the Whipple Hollow settlers used to bring in their corn, grateful for the service that Sutherland was only too glad to give.

Undoubtedly the mills had a greater bearing on Sutherland's prosperity than he was ever permitted to see. That he was on the Green Mountain Boys' questionable list has never been denied. It has been hinted that they were more than once at the point of driving him away from his holdings but that each time he was finally allowed to remain because the settlers were depending on him for lumber and meal. Whatever may have been the condition, neither his person nor his property was ever molested. The wheels in his mills continued to drone out their welcome and his domain was extended until he owned all the land on the west side of the Creek between the Pittsford line and what was later recognized as the northern border of the Mead farm. Within a very few years his settlement had taken its place as the pivotal point of the Sutherland Falls section.

By the time Sutherland was well established at the Great Falls, there was a clearing cut away near the Little Falls where the village of Center Rutland had its origin. This work was being done by Col. James Mead of Manchester. He had previously moved into the state from Nine Partners, N. Y., and on becoming interested in the Rutland territory he bought a large tract of land and immediately began to plan for his conquest of the wilderness. The spot he selected for his cabin was at the fork of the highways where the road turns north on the west side of the river.

In the spring of 1770 Colonel Mead, with a family that numbered twelve, toiled up through the valley toward the half-completed cabin which had been raised the preceding fall. They had been three days on the road from Manchester, camping the first night in Dorset and the second in Danby. It was late in the day when they sighted their new home and it was an unalterably cheerless view which met their eyes. Winter had left the roofless cabin in a sorry condition.

Indians were encamped nearby and the disheartened emigrants, intent on procuring shelter for the night, appealed to them for a share in their fire-illumined wigwam. After talking together for a few moments in their guttural language, the redmen gave the sign of welcome. More than that, they went outside and built another wigwam for their sleeping place, leaving the first retreat for the undivided use of the strangers. In these meager quarters the Mead family remained until the following autumn when a new log cabin was ready for their occupancy. Although the

James Mead settlement has no direct connection with
the town of Proctor it is not without interest, nor indeed did it fail to wield an influence on the Sutherland
Falls community. From it grew the village of Center
Rutland, the forerunner of Rutland City. The Mead
house at Little Falls became a well known stopping
place for the passing traveler, taking upon itself the
rather pretentious title of Mead's Tavern. Even now
one may locate the old well which was once at the service of the grateful wayfarers. As for the proprietor of
the Tavern, his name appears more than once in the
early chronicles of the state, not alone in military
affairs but in the none the less perilous activities of the
Dorset and Windsor conventions.

Within the fifty-year period dating ahead from
1770 there were less than a score of homes added to
the territory that has since been chartered as the town
of Proctor. Yet each of these original clearings is in
itself a compelling bit of history, revealing a story re-
plete with all the fascinating elements of a romance.
Some of them were long ago obliterated; others are
marked only by an indistinct grass-carpeted cellar-hole.
There can be no better way than to take them in order
and relate some of the incidents which tradition has
fastened upon them.

While Colonel Mead was housing his family in
the Indian wigwam, Captain Doolittle the promoter
of the Pittsford charter was urging his brother-in-law,
Roger Stevens of Quaker Hill, N. Y., to take up land
in the river country. Heeding the captain's advice,
the Stevens household decided to emigrate to Pittsford,
where land was cheap and unsubdued. Once there the
head of the family with the help of his sons rimmed out
a little spot in the woods and marked it with a house.

CELLAR HOLE OF ROGER STEVENS' CABIN, BUILT IN 1770

This cabin was set on the crest of the hill about thirty rods west of Gorham Bridge and bounded on the north by the Crown Point road. The cellar over which it was constructed is now open to the sky and two stalwart butternut trees have grown within its walls.

Roger Stevens was of Welch descent, his father having sailed for this country early in the eighteenth century. The young Roger, when he was fit for work, was made an apprentice to a hatter and until the trade was learned and for some years thereafter he continued in the business. On transferring his possessions to Pittsford he went at the oaks and evergreens with similar tenacity. As time went on the land about the cabin was shorn of its trees, the acres being transformed into food-producing fields.

Steven's life in the community seems to have been more or less of an enigma. It is known that one of his sons, Roger Stevens, Jr., joined the British forces at the outbreak of the war, and was a continual trouble-maker for the Revolutionary forces. On entering the service, he left his family at Pittsford to care for the new home they had established, and during the years of his absence he sometimes visited them, coming and going under the secrecy of night. In this manner he was enabled to take back with him a liberal amount of data that was exceedingly useful to the enemy. The Vermont authorities, through the confiscation and sale of his lands, finally prevailed on him to discontinue his visits. Both Roger Stevens, Jr., and his father spent their last days in Canada.

Another homestead which had its beginning in 1770 was the one founded by Samuel Crippen. It lay still farther up the hill west of Gorham bridge, a holding of land that later generations have christened the "Old

Shangraw Place." In common with many of the Connecticut families, the Crippens originated in England
and were among the earliest to seek the freedom of the
Colonial shores. Their estate in the Otter Creek valley
was purchased of James Mead, the sale taking place
in midsummer, allowing time before cold weather for
the welding of some of the trees into a house. And thus
it came about in the fall that Samuel Crippen and his
wife took up the work of keeping alive another oasis in
the desert forest. Could they have foreseen the perilous
times through which they were to fight their way, it is
quite possible that the first fire on their hearthstone
might also have been the last.

For a time their lot was no more thrilling than the
common round of frontier life. The great adventure
came in the summer of 1781. Mr. Crippen left his
work in the hayfield and started on foot for Fort Vengeance in Pittsford. On reaching a neighbor's house
he accepted the loan of a horse and saddle. A little
farther on he was overpowered by a Tory-directed band
of Indians and borne away toward Canada a prisoner,
leaving the hastily summoned relief party far in the
rear. It was the rumor of the day that the Tory in question was none other than Roger Stevens, Jr., the son
of Crippen's nearest neighbor.

The months of Canadian captivity, while they
were never free from hardship and indignity, had an
ending far more propitious than the average Indian
experience. Within a year the white man was given
his liberty and the right to return to the Vermont
Grants on parole. As a precaution against a second
forced march into the north country he at once moved
his belongings to Wallingford, a town which was better
able to resist the depredations of the redmen. At the

time of his departure he looked ahead to the day when the land should be at peace and he could make a second start in his old home. But that day proved to be little better than a will-o-the-wisp. Mr. Crippen died in Wallingford in 1783.

Nothing now remains of the original Crippen buildings, although there are certain older residents who can remember when some of them were intact. It is believed that a part of the timber taken out of the earlier structure was worked into the Shangraw property. The years were not many that Samuel Crippen spent almost within sight of Sutherland Falls, yet they were full of industry and they were enough to assure the newcomer a place as a man of character. His name is among those listed in 1773 as members of the First Congregational Church of Rutland.

Nor was the family name one that passed out with the first generation. A son, Amos Crippen, was the builder of what eventually became the Lewis White place, and of a shop nearby in which he toiled for many years as a blacksmith.

Another relative, David Crippen, bought twenty acres of the land previously relinquished by Colonel Mead, and on that soil was shaped another opening and another home. This latter cabin, a product of 1774, was about six rods west of the Otter Creek and forty or fifty rods south of Gorham Bridge.

David Crippen began operations in February. In the fall of that year, Ezra Mead and Henry, his grandson, drove their cattle up the valley and set up camp on the lowlands which from that day to this have been under the control of the Mead family. Zebulon, the father of Henry, and a brother of James Mead, was to have joined them later in the season, bringing with him

By His Excellency

The Honourable ROBERT MONCKTON, Captain

General and Governor in Chief, in and over the Province of New-York, and the Territories depending thereon in America, Vice Admiral of the fame, and Major General of His Majefty's Forces.

● To *Zebulon Mead Esq Greeting*

REPOSING efpecial Truft and Confidence, as well in the Care, Diligence, and Circumfpection, as in the Loyalty, Courage and Readinefs of You, to do His Majefty good and faithful Service; HAVE nominated, conftitued and appointed, and I DO, hereby by Virtue of the Powers and Authorities to Me given by His Majefty, hereby nominate, conftitute and appoint You the faid *Zebulon Mead to Captain of the Company* ~~of Militia Foot lately commanded by Captain Nathan Smith deceased in the North Battalion of the Regiment for the County of Dutches whereof Morlin Beekman Esq is Colonel~~

You are therefore to take the faid *Company* into your Charge and Care, as *Captain* in Arms. And thereof, and duly to exercife both the Officers and Soldiers of that *Company* + in Arms. And as they are hereby commanded to obey You as their *Captain* for to are You likewife to obferve and follow fuch Orders and Directions, from time to time, as You fhall receive from Me, or any other your Superior Officer, according to the Rules and Difcipline of War, in Purfuance of the Truft repofed in You; and for fo doing, this fhall be your Commiffion.

GIVEN under my Hand, and Seal at Arms, in New-York, the *twenty Ninth* Day of *October* in the *Third* Year of His Majefty's Reign, Annoq; Domini, One Thoufand Seven Hundred and Sixty*two*

Wm Monckton

By His Excellency's Command,

ZEBULON MEAD COMMISSION

the other members of the household and a store of provisions, but for some undisclosed reason the start was delayed until the following spring. This left the two stock-tenders to pass the winter alone amid strange and cheerless surroundings. The cabin which they fashioned down by the creek was rough and open-jointed, a poor barricade against the chill of the marshes. Their only clothing was of linen weave, and their food supply was even more scanty than their wearing apparel. Nor was there anything for the cattle to eat save what could be gathered from bushes. Then, as a climax to the long round of hardships, the spring rains brought the river up over its banks, flooding the cabin and forc-ing both men and animals to swim for the higher ground.

That summer, the united family, profiting by first year lessons, pitched a second cabin on their newly pur-chased land. Its cellar was considerably above the river level and a little south of the site now claimed by the brick house. This was the last cabin to rise on the estate. From there the Meads moved across the road to a real farm house. In later years the men who have ploughed the fields east of the brick homestead have brought to light a variety of knives, hatchets and other implements, all rusty with age and exposure, the rem-nants of that earlier home which faced the sunset.

The first ancestors of the Mead family came to England in the wake of the Norman conquest. William Mead, the father of the Vermont branch, sailed for America in 1635. During the subsequent years there were a series of migrations, a cycle which began at Stamford, Conn., and swung around through Nine Partners, New York, to the final stand on the shores of the Otter. In all their wanderings the fighting spirit of old Normandy was still burning within them. There was little chance for it to smoulder. They were thrown first into the vortex of Indian fighting, then into the more systematic service of Revolutionary days. The original army commissions, awarded to Capt. Zebulon Mead in 1762 and to Henry Mead in 1790 and 1791, are still counted the choicest heirlooms of the old West Road dwelling.

Northwest of the Mead settlement, on a trail which slants up the mountain side, is a capacious spring, one that was known to the Indians long before it was ferreted out by the white men. The water has certain mineral properties which to the Indian were of very definite medicinal value, and tribesmen from both north and south have gathered in solemn conclave around its forest-cooled basin. It was their custom at such times to drink unsparingly, that they might be the better able to withstand disease. If there happened to be a sick man in camp he was bundled on to a horse and made a part of the procession, so that he too could be brought within touch of the health-mending pool. This spring was wrapped in superstition; from the first it was set apart as neutral ground. The tribesmen from different sections were oftentimes the most vindictive of enemies, but there at the water's edge they put aside their animosities and kept the peace.

The path to the spring was a part of the longer course which reached over the top of the mountain, and in the terrorized flight which grew out of the Battle of Hubbardton, the refugees stormed down its narrow, forest-enclosed recesses, never once halting until they were within call of the Mead stockade. They stopped there to sound a warning and to declare that the Indians would soon be upon them, and then they rushed on toward Bennington. The members of the Mead family, having no desire to take part in an Indian celebration, assembled some of their belongings in an ox cart, and burying the crockery and a few other things of weight and value in the river, they set out after the fleeing caravan on the road to Center Rutland. Hardly were they under way when the axle broke, compelling them to abandon the cart. The best they could then do was to tie the bedding to the backs of the oxen, and with this as a seat for the women, the outcasts finally stalked into Bennington, there to remain until the battle* had been fought outside the town and the fear of invasion was no longer running wild.

It was stated by Governor Clinton of New York that, "after the battle at Bennington, not an Indian was heard to the northward; the scalping business seemed to have ceased."

In later years when the track was being laid for the Clarendon & Pittsford railroad, one of the laborers drove his spade down into the mouldy log-ribbed wall of the old Mead stockade. He was digging about forty rods south of the Mead place and a little west of the highway. Anyone who would question the wisdom of building a fort on low approachable ground should review the conditions under which this was brought into service. The river was the Indian waterway. In time of danger the pioneers could gather in the stockade and watch the movements of the enemy up and down the creek, and with the military road passing the door and the high hills near at hand, they could the more readily communicate with their neighbors. When no

* Accounts of the Battle of Bennington refer to James Claghorn, whose name often appears in the early land records of the Sutherland Falls country. It is said of him that he came out of that conflict with six bullet holes in his hat.

To *Henry Mead Gentleman* — — — — *Greeting.*

You being elected *Lieutenant of the 1st Company 8th Regiment*

1st — — — — Brigade of the Militia of this State:

repoſing ſpecial Truſt and Confidence in your Patriciſm, Valour and good Conduct, I DO, by Virtue of theſe Preſents, in the Name and by the Authority of the State of *VERMONT*, fully authoriſe and empower you the ſaid *Henry*

to take Charge of ſaid *Company* — as their *Lieutenant*. You will

therefore carefully and diligently diſcharge the ſaid Duty, by doing and performing all and every Matter and Thing thereunto relating:
You will obſerve and follow ſuch Orders and Directions as you ſhall from Time to Time receive from me, the Governor of the
State for the Time being, or any other your ſuperior Officers, according to military Rules and Diſcipline, and the Laws of the State.
And all Officers and Soldiers under your Command, are to take Notice hereof, and yield due Obedience to your Orders as
in purſuance of the Truſt in you repoſed.

GIVEN under my Hand, and the Seal of this State, at *Council*, dated the *9th* — — Day of *Sept* 1792.

By his EXCELLENCY'S Command,

Joseph Fay Secy

Moses Robinson

HENRY MEAD COMMISSION

other outlets were open, there were the mountains with their signal fires as an agency for the forwarding of news. Even brief signs were welcome when they flashed a warning; it was everything just to know which way the redskins were moving.

There were three of the Mead brothers who had a hand in the settlement of Rutland county; Zebulon at Sutherland Falls, James whose entry into Rutland has already been described, and Stephen who bought from James a holding north of the Samuel Crippen right and so became one of the fathers of Pittsford. The efforts of this family in the upbuilding of the community were constant and varied. Undeniably, the first need of the town was for men who could fight. No settlement could hope to keep itself on the map unless its veins were vibrant with strength and aggressiveness. But when the right to existence began to pass unchallenged there was a call for constructive work, for officers who could bring the settlers together within the circle of a local government. In this latter service, as well as in the exigencies of warfare, the Meads were ardent and loyal contributors.

Following the Meads there was no further extension of the settlement until 1777. In January of that year, Stephen Mead transferred one hundred acres of Pittsford land to John May, a newcomer at the Grants. May was an Englishman, born in 1746, who sailed for America when but a youth. His holdings in Vermont included nearly all of the farm which subsequently became the property of Lewis White. His house, which grew to completion in the spring, was a little southwest of the Roger Stevens place. The cellar was still intact as late as 1872, and could no doubt be located even now by the large boulder which was the homestead's birthmark. The old road which curled around the Lewis White place to the door of the May cabin, and then on toward Sutherland Falls, is no longer a public highway, although its bed is still set apart by scattering posts. For several years May retained his proprietorship and committed himself to the varying fortunes of his rocky estate. As to the actual length of his stay on the place, or where he again threw out the latch string, there is little that can be said.

In 1777 also there arrived James Ewing, who bought fifty acres of unreclaimed land of Darius Crippen and chopped out a place large enough for a cabin. This land lay to the southward from the original David Crippen property and was then in possession of the son Darius. Other land was added to Ewing's estate from time to time and from it finally emerged the A. C. Powers farm. Indeed one need only have walked across the road toward the west from the house that old residents still look back upon as the A. C. Powers place, to stand on the identical spot where that first settler framed his log hut.

James Ewing, by the way, was a son-in-law of Benjamin Cooley, one of the two brothers who lived the first chapter in the history of Pittsford.

The coming of Isaac Chatterton was the event of 1783. The land which he brought under the swing of his plough was on the east side of the river, across from the Mead farm. No doubt there is somewhere a yellowed book which would tell how he acquired the title to the ancestral acres, but no one seems to know where it is, nor has anything been disclosed relative to his early life or the trail which led him down amid the storms and vicissitudes of the river country. Whatever may have been his motive in taking up his residence in the valley, there was nothing at all questionable about his years of service or the integrity of purpose which lay behind them. When he died the homestead was bequeathed to his only son. It was that son, Leverett Chatterton, who built the old stone house which is serving today as a home for the town's poor. A little south-east from the stone house, and on the other side of the road, is another and an older Chatterton building, older even though it may have been remodeled by a later generation of carpenters.

To read of the early years of the Humphrey family is like going to the library shelves and turning the pages of some old romance. Joseph Humphrey, the founder, was born at Winchester, N. H., the son of Colonel William Humphrey, a Revolutionary officer. There were fifteen children in the family and as they began to grow it was inevitable that the parental cabin should feel the strain. While still six years under the freeman's age, Joseph went out in search of more room. He left Winchester in 1784, his only clothing on his back, his only luggage the axe which was flung over his shoulder. His feet were bare and he wore no coat. Alone and unencumbered, he crossed the Connecticut and turned northward up into the Green Mountain wilds, asking for nothing but an opportunity to carve out a place for himself.

The chance came when he arrived at Sutherland Falls. Someone set him at work and he kept at it. A part of his labor went into the building of the old stone jail at Rutland. Then he moved north up the Otter. Isaac Chatterton was another of his employers and so was John Sutherland. Nine years of toil and planning and saving, and he had raised himself from the ranks of the hired men to the company of the property owners.

MILLS IN 1885

He was able to negotiate with Sutherland for the transfer of sixty acres bordering on the river and reaching south to the Mead line. Thus was the Humphrey farm given its name and brought under family sovereignty.

There was a log cabin on the property, one that nobody seemed to want. It had been left there alone until it was in very truth a part of the forest. Young saplings were crowding in from without and a misguided sumach had sprung up in the earthen fireplace and was even then thrusting its branches out into the light. It was two years before young Humphrey had redeemed the premises to his liking, and then, one day, an ox sled came creaking up to the door, heralding the arrival of a young lady on horseback—the first Humphrey bride at Sutherland Falls.

The coming of Hannah Parmalee of Pittsford and the conversion of the homely cabin into a real home, has been quaintly set forth in manuscript form by one of the descendants of that first family. The paper cannot now be located but its lines have been interwoven with several of the town histories, gaining thereby a recognized standing among the community traditions. The moving on that long ago winter's day was all accomplished at one load, and even so the sled was not overtaxed. Two brothers of the bride had joined the party, so that there might be someone to drive back the oxen. And so there were four to sit down to supper on the day the new housekeeper came.

It was a very frugal meal and it was served in true picnic fashion. Bread was brought in from the load, and, since the young husband had already laid in a stock of pork and corn meal, a johnny cake was soon baking beside the fire and the aroma of fried ham began to steal out into the clearing. There were only three chairs and three knives and forks in the cabin, so it was imperative that Joseph Humphrey should eat with a jack-knife and a wooden fork and use a block of wood for a dining chair. In these days no one would think of starting under so formidable a handicap, yet it was accepted by the pioneers as the inevitable beginning, out of which they must build the prosperity of the coming years.

After about two years of toil and good management, Joseph Humphrey was able to raise a frame house and turn his back on the clumsy log cabin. This second home flaunted one and a half stories. It looked out to the south from a point nearly 175 feet east, or slightly northeast, of the brick homestead that has been the birthplace of later generations. In this more commodious and comfortable dwelling, the founder of the Humphrey family lived the greater portion of his life, and, under the watchful eye of his good wife, several sturdy children were made ready to take their places in the world.

The brick house that now stands guard over the Humphrey acres was completed in 1826. It was constructed by William Humphrey, the eldest of Joseph's sons. Its walls were in line with the four points of the compass, in recognition of the builder's activities as a land surveyor. It was an unusual structure in that practically all the materials out of which it was formed were produced within the boundaries of the estate. Trees of course were waiting for the axe and saw, and down across the road to the west was a kiln where the bricks were made. To the eastward was an outcropping ledge of marble, a ledge which in the passing of time became the nucleus of the Columbian quarry, and from this bed were wedged out the slabs with which the windows were trimmed. Even the nails might have been of home manufacture, for on the high ledge north of the projected cellar was an iron deposit of known and tested character.

The old house remained intact until the latter part of the nineteenth century, but it was robbed of its prestige when the larger home took its place in the foreground. Indeed, this new abode of the Humphrey family was unique among the other buildings of the settlement. It was the first to have its walls formed of brick. Later it was forced to share the distinction with others, but in the beginning it was the only representative of its class, set apart by all the exclusiveness that is usually accorded to a leader.

The original Humphrey farm was bounded on the north by the Beaver Pond Brook, a little stream that is now out of sight under the marble yards. The western corner stones were at the top of West Mountain. Looking out over such an expanse, the home of William Humphrey was provided with a setting which no man could criticise. It included the level part of the valley, the section from which later generations were to harvest a long succession of crops; it included also the unnumbered oaks and spruces that were deeply rooted in every acre. Near one of those primeval spruces, in the pasture to the rear of the house, is the site of the family burying ground. The bodies were all removed to a Pittsford cemetery many years ago, yet the ragged, wind-frayed spruce still holds itself erect, in remembrance of the days and the lives that are gone.

It was only a few years after the Sutherlands sold the land south of Beaver Brook to the Humphreys, that they transferred the territory on the north to R. M. Powers, whose first holdings in the settlement were

MILLS AND VILLAGE IN 1900

far up in the northwest corner, on a stretch of hillside that has since been defined as the "Old Wright Place." Mr. Powers was born in Greenwich, Mass., on Christmas Day, 1775. He arrived at the outposts of Pittsford in about 1792 with an eye open for the opportunities which were said to be knocking at every cabin door. Three years apparently was enough to give him a start, for in 1795 he bought his first real estate and began cultivating and improving it. Before winter closed in he had completed a house on the property. Then came his marriage to Polly Carpenter of Chittenden, followed in the spring by the opening of their first home in the Pittsford valley.

That home stood on the west side of the road, up over the hill from the Roger Stevens place and a little southwest from the John May clearing. The crumbling walls may still be located if one knows where to look—a pile of cellar stones over which the weeds and undergrowth drape themselves at will. It is only a few rods east of the Clarendon & Pittsford railroad track, and almost equally distant from the old Market Highway. One might travel far to find a more sightly spot, but it is quite possible that the scenery may have been better than the soil. In any event, Mr. Powers only retained his ownership a little more than a year, the title being transferred in 1797 to Robert Wright. Shortly afterward, the retiring claimant made a second investment and became the proprietor of the James Ewing farm, a holding which has already been described. For a few years he banked his fires under the original Ewing roof, then he mortised together the larger Powers' dwelling on the other side of the road, which was to be passed down to his children as a lasting tribute to his foresight and thoroughness.

When Peter Sutherland decided to pull up stakes at the Falls and part with the claim which had been his father's best venture, it was R. M. Powers who stood first among the buyers. Papers were signed which relinquished all Sutherland control to that unbroken group of hills and hollows on which the entire northern part of the village of Proctor was to rise. With the land went the water rights at the Falls and an old building near at hand. With it too went a matchless deposit of marble although neither party to the contract had any inkling of the fact. And in later years Mr. Powers sold to Forbes Manley fifteen acres of that land, the very ground on which the Sutherland Falls quarry was finally opened, for the extremely nominal consideration of forty-five dollars. In that period the things of greatest industrial moment were all on top of the earth; few of the settlers had any time to waste on the uncertainties that lurked underground. The successor to the Sutherland business organization at the Falls continued to court prosperity after the manner of his predecessor, interesting himself now and then in a shop or a mill and buying and selling land whenever the right kind of prospect could be located. Perhaps, after all, it was best that the value of the marble beds remained an unguessed secret. The hour had not struck when Vermont quarries could be profitably operated, nor was it to be sounded for many a long year. As it was, the well-rounded life of R. M. Powers was never distorted by any of the quarrying experiments that crippled the pioneers of the marble industry. What lay beneath his feet never had the chance to breed longing and discontent because there was no one to tell him about it.

Right here a line must be drawn between the eighteenth and nineteenth centuries. For a space of nine years no settlements were made; in fact, there were only five or six newcomers during the next quarter century. These arrivals should be introduced separately, since to each of them belongs an individual niche in the town's hall of fame.

In 1804, Morris Reynolds moved over the line and planted his hearthstone near the Double Roads Crossing. His father, Jonathan Reynolds, was even then an established resident of the valley, although the smoke from his fireplace was farther to the south, so that it has no logical place in these records. The land had been deeded to him by Col. James Mead. It centered upon the eastern side of the Creek on soil that townspeople of a later day recognize as the Grafton Griggs farm. The date of transfer must be classed with the uncertainties, but the matter of price seems to be somewhat less obscure. It is maintained by one of the family descendants that Colonel Mead was induced to part with the entire estate of 275 acres in exchange for three or four otter skins, a transaction which reverts very forcefully to the relative values of land and otter skins. It seems that the elder Reynolds had been commissioned as a lieutenant in the Revolutionary Army, and that, on leaving the service, his activities as a hunter and trapper brought him more or less local renown. One might suppose that, for a man of that type, a property so extensive, secured through the delivery of a few otters, would be a rare bargain. However that may have been regarded, the Reynolds homestead was thus instituted, and there it was that Morris Reynolds passed the maturing years of his life. As already related, he hung out a latchstring of his own in 1804. Other sons and daughters also detached themselves from the parent nest and made other homes in the valley. Still

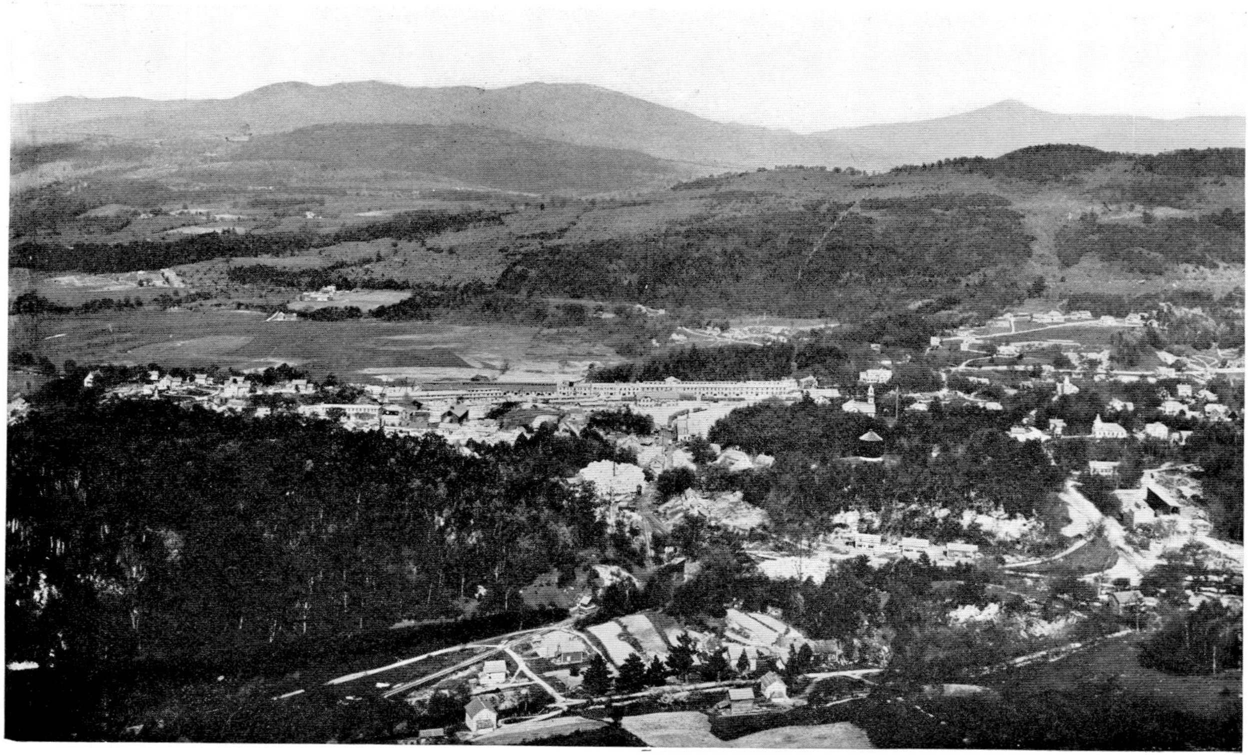

MILLS AND VILLAGE IN 1910

Jonathan Reynolds clung to the house he knew best. For thirty-six years he traveled on in the old way. When, in 1840, there came to his ears the call that cannot be ignored, he lacked only sixteen days of being one hundred years old.

The year 1811 brought another worker to the settlement in the person of Benjamin Capron. One may still inspect the timbers which he drew out of the forest and fitted into the old house on the West Road. His estate has never relinquished its right to be called the Capron place; it has been carried down from one Capron family to another throughout the round of the century. A second place of the same name, over which one of the first sons presided, was maintained for a time a few rods to the northward, but it was finally reduced to ashes and has never been rebuilt.

In the records of the town of Rutland is the copy of a deed in which Adam Hinsman, of Southbury, Conn., conveyed to Benjamin McIntire sixty acres of land. It is likewise recorded that Caleb Whipple, of Rutland, deeded to Benjamin McIntire two tracts, including the Falls of the Otter Creek, which he had previously purchased of Peter Sutherland. Looking through these musty pages back into the past we get the impression that Mr. McIntire, whatever else he may have lacked, was well provided with land and water. He chose as his headquarters a little square of ground, bordering on the South street of later years. Perhaps even now in Robert McGregor's cellar are some of the same stones which the earlier settler collected, for the one foundation rose upon the decayed, blackened ruins of the other. The McIntire structure burned in the early forties. The barn lay to the south of the house where now the Catholic rectory raises its head above the trees.

There is no one to tell us as to when and where Benjamin McIntire died, and his land has long since been
divided up into building lots and ball grounds and
cemeteries. Warner's Grove was once a part of his estate.

Twelve years after acquiring this Sutherland Falls
property he deeded his entire farm to his daughter,
Sarah Ann McIntire, who was the wife of Jesse Paul.
A little postscript was added to the contract stating
that whenever the daughter and son-in-law failed to
provide suitably for the McIntire family, the deed
should become void. Apparently this was a rare expression of foresight, for at the expiration of three
years the farm was deeded back to the father. In describ-
ing the boundary line there is reference inevitably to
the usual number of dry pines, white oaks, and sticks
and stones, but we are informed also that it was bounded on the south by Isaac Chatterton's land and on the
north by the land of Israel Pennock, all three properties being on the east bank of the Otter Creek.

This man Pennock was another of the town's
pioneers. He bought his first real estate of Benjamin
McIntire in 1813 and between that year and 1818 he
made four additions to it. In 1817 he bargained with
Peter Sutherland for a five acre plot and reared a house
thereon, the house which gave way in turn to. the
Ormsbee dwelling and the Proctor Memorial Library.
Let it not be understood that the Library has the same
relative position as the Pennock cabin. On the con-
trary, the older landmark was several rods to the northward. According to no less an authority than Mr. Hamilton Ormsbee, a son who was born and reared there
where the road turns down to the bridge, the kitchen
of the little Ormsbee cottage was moved over from the
flat at the top of Patch Hill. He remembers that in his

boyhood days the spot was disfigured by an old cellar hole. That undoubtedly was the hole in which Israel Pennock grounded his chimney. The tradition is that the first religious service in town was opened in Mr. Pennock's barn, which was situated across the road and farther up the hill near the Fletcher Proctor residence.

Reverting again to that McIntire deed, we learn that a part of East Mountain was then owned by Chauncy D. Tuttle. How long he had been there is another one of the uncertainties. Let us give him the benefit of the doubt, assuming that he arrived prior to 1820, and so grant him a place in the first division of the town's progenitors. Back of the ball grounds at Warner's Grove is a sightly knoll, indented with what must have once been the cellar of the Tuttle house. It was old when the settlement was young. There it was that N. S. Warner, father of Myron Warner, lived while the Peter Morganson house was being finished.

Of another old cellar farther up the mountain— the one which has raised to maturity a gigantic butter-nut tree—still less is known. It is past the halfway mark on the climb to the summit and almost directly east from the railway station. Rumor has it that the house which once kept it company was the home of Jesse Paul, McIntire's son-in-law, but rumor at best is poor history, so really there is no reason why Paul should be dragged into this paragraph.

In the old burying ground at Center Rutland, closed in by the railroad and the highway, are the graves of Leverett Chatterton, Israel Pennock and Jesse Paul. Anyone who cares to dig into the wild rose briars and dead grass may read the marble slabs— tablets which were placed there, so the inscriptions tell us, in the years 1827, 1829 and 1852.

MILLS AND VILLAGE IN 1922

The first farm north of Cummings Manor is now called the Wilkins farm, but back in 1869 it was known as the Nahum Johnson place. Still farther back, in 1813, when it was built, and for many years thereafter, its title was in the hands of John Johnson. Johnson, senior, was one of those who came up from the Saybrook Colony, Connecticut, in ox teams. In 1773 he rolled into West Rutland, and there he remained for forty-six years, until the house on the West Road opened its doors to admit him. During this time he became prominent in the community both as a man and a public official. The same fidelity and good judgment which had made him an efficient soldier in the Revolutionary period, gave him exceptional capacity in other lines.

To write again of the days of seventy-six is to recall that while these primal families were converting the wilderness into something a little less somber and threatening, the country at large was throwing off its coat and buckling down to the business of making a name for itself. Not only had it finished the Revolution triumphantly but another war as well.*

Vermont had been admitted to the Union and was making of herself a creditable unit, and one which insisted on being heard. Even little Sutherland Falls

---

*When, in September, 1814, the call was relayed down the valley for volunteers to take part in the Battle of Plattsburg, two of the Falls men who responded were R. M. Powers and his son, Richard Montgomery, second. With others from this section they tramped to the lake front, all except Tilly Walker, who was one of the wagoners, halting finally at a point north of Burlington on the banks of the Winooski River. There they were obliged to remain, for the boat which was to have borne them across the lake was late in arriving. They heard the thunder of the guns, and that was all. It was while they were waiting there on the Vermont side that R. M. Powers, the younger, lost his life. Blind to the strong under-current. he dove into the river for a swim and was swept over the falls to his death, His grave is in the Burlington cemetery, near the spot where the body of Ethan Allen was laid away.

was represented at the council fires by its own favored sons of the forest. The rifle trade was still good but no longer was it the all-absorbing thing. Public welfare came in for casual notice. There were dreams of industrial development.

Notice this paragraph taken from Mason's History:

"By the year 1794, settlement had so far progressed and stock accumulated that it was deemed necessary to order that sheep and swine should not be permitted to run at large. Bridges had been built at Sutherland Falls and Reynold's Mill, and these were ordered repaired if needed. One hundred and twenty-five pounds of powder, three hundred and fifty-four of lead, and four hundred and fifty flints were also ordered purchased; indicating that the warlike spirit engendered by the Revolution was still abroad."

On the other hand the records show that, as late as 1818, Peter Sutherland conveyed by deed to Solomon Gill of Rutland the sole water rights on the east side of Sutherland Falls. The paper was written with all the legal flourishes which the transfer of a continent might demand. It was majestically set forth that Peter Sutherland proposed to "give, grant, bargain, sell and confirm unto the said Solomon, his heirs and assigns forever, all the rights and privileges, et cetera." And for what consideration? For the lofty sum of eight dollars. It must be inferred therefore that while there may have been dreams of industrial expansion in 1818 they were so far removed from realities as to keep the price of power sites ridiculously low. In these days eight dollars would be hardly enough to pay for the writing of the contract.

CHAPTER III

GROWTH OF THE SETTLEMENT—1820-1849

BUILDING HIGHWAYS AND BRIDGES—NEW HOUSES
ERECTED—INDUSTRIAL DEVELOPMENT—SOCIAL
CUSTOMS—THE COMING OF THE RAILROAD—
DIFFICULTIES OF CONSTRUCTION—FIRST
TRAIN—MIKE EAGAN

THE story of the Military Road has already
been told. That was the initial wedge in the
opening of the wilderness. In a similar way the
other highways, constructed from time to time, gave
fresh incentive to the work of stabilizing the settlement.
They were not much like the easily traversed thorough-
fares of today. Indeed they were little more than
tunnels cut through the almost unlimited woodland.

As it appears in Caverly's History of Pittsford
"the early roads in the township, like those in other
parts of the new country, were little better than rude
paths in the wilderness. A narrow passage was made
by cutting away trees and bushes, and streams that
could not be easily forded were bridged with logs. No
turnpike welcomed the weary travelers and no toll-
gatherer laid him under contribution; his progress was
measured by his strength and power of muscular
endurance."

Yet these paths, crude though they were, be-
tokened an advancing civilization. The settlers reas-
oned, even as the people of today, that living near a

poor road is better than having none at all within reach. And so each fresh channel in the forest became a magnet, drawing unto itself a broken line of cabins.

In the Laws of Vermont for 1806 there is an act which appoints and instructs a committee "to lay out and survey a market road, the most convenient and direct route to Troy in the state of New York, beginning at or near Stephen Hard's Esquire's in Salisbury, thence through the towns of Leicester, Brandon and Pittsford until it intersects the road that leads from Rutland to Castleton."

This became known as the Market Road. It passed through Sutherland Falls on the west side of Otter Creek. It is nearest approximated today by the road which runs from Brandon to Florence, then past the Lewis White place and Beaver Pond, continuing on to the Rutland line. This, so far as it had to do with Sutherland Falls, was virtually a duplication of the old Military Highway. The chief purpose in opening it was to provide that section of country around Salisbury with a market outlet, since that part of the valley had been left in isolation when the military turnpike swerved off to the westward.

In the course of time little branches were pushed out from this parent stem. It is a well-grounded tradition that one of these offshoots trailed up over the crest of East Mountain. Another switched off at the Humphrey place, wound up through the sugar wood and the hollow south of the parsonage, turning up the hill north of the Union Church and coming out at the Sutherland house. Another looped around through the knolls and hollows which are now covered by the marble yards, crossing the brook from Beaver Pond and joining the Sutherland Mills with the Market Road.

The Proctor Road Book contains surveys of the valley road between Rutland and Pittsford, one section of which was laid out in 1807 and the other in 1816, both on the east side of Otter Creek. The survey of 1807 led up the mountain at the foot of Patch Hill, and curved around by the Tuttle house, dropping down to the lower level again near the Dodge farm.

In the old Pittsford records we read that in the south part of the town a road was laid out extending from the Military Road a little east of the residence of Gideon Cooley to the Great Falls. Also that another road was laid out from Mr. Cooley's to Otter Creek near the residence of Roger Stevens. A crossing was made there, sometimes upon a jam of logs which then existed and sometimes in a boat.

This recalls the early experiences of the pioneers in the arduous work of bridge building. It is apparent that bridges gave little trouble to the first road makers simply because they left them out of the plan. It was the path through the forest that counted; the river could be forded. The most the traveler could expect when he reached the water was that the stream was fordable, otherwise the trail would not have approached it at that point.

It is uncertain as to where the first bridge timbers of the Valley were set in place, but this much is known. There was a framed structure of some sort stretched across the Otter on the site of the Proctor Memorial Bridge as early as 1794. It went out in the great flood of 1811. A second one was soon in place and this was carried over the falls in 1839 as a result of defective stone work in the foundation.

This catastrophe is clearly recalled by Mrs. Mary Wheeler Wright of Brandon. At that time she was

THE OLD COVERED BRIDGE

attending school in the old Library Building, now the Municipal Memorial. Mrs. Hills Taylor, mother of B. F. Taylor, was her teacher. Her people were then living in the Pennock, or Ormsbee house. After a part of the bridge had gone over the falls her uncle, S. B. Loveland, came to get her and he carried her home across the river balancing himself on the few timbers that were still left in place. Mrs. Wright remembers that the abutments of the bridge had been displaced by ice. In this latter emergency Hills Taylor, the father of B. F. Taylor, opened the way to traffic by hauling beams across the river with a four-horse team.

Yet this was only a temporary makeshift and for a time there was a break in the road at Sutherland's. Miss Julia Humphrey tells of a daughter of Israel Pennock who was drowned in 1840 while attempting to cross the river in a boat. Since there was no bridge a young man offered to pilot her to the other side. But in some way the boat was overturned and although the man finally reached the shore he was unable to save the girl.

In 1841 came the covered bridge which was to serve the public until the advent of the marble arches in 1915. It was constructed by Lewis Wolcott of Pittsford.

While Wolcott was wrestling with his overhead tunnel above Sutherland Falls, Nicholas Powers, the uncle of Harry P. Powers, acting as inspector for the town of Rutland, was building the Gorham bridge below the falls. He had previously pinned together the covered bridge at Pittsford Mills. These two products of his hand are standing today, having reached the good old age of four-score years. The achievement takes on added glamor when it is revealed that Powers had never even seen a covered bridge when he took the contract at Pittsford Mills.

MARBLE MEMORIAL BRIDGE WHICH REPLACED THE OLD COVERED BRIDGE

It was to be his fortune to see many more before he died. He became known the country over for his work along those lines. At Blenheim, N. Y., he raised a single-span wooden bridge that was 231 feet between abutments, the largest single span on record at that time. In 1866 he superintended the framing of a bridge across the Susquehanna in Maryland which was seven-eighths of a mile in length.

In passing it should be noted that the first bridge at Sutherland Falls, which by the way was known as the Union Bridge, was destroyed by the great flood of 1811. This is described very picturesquely by Dr. Caverly of Pittsford.

"About the 11th of July occurred one of the most remarkable floods that has ever visited this section of the country. It commenced early in the morning with a succession of thunder showers. Towards noon the clouds gathered blackness, the rain descended in torrents and during the afternoon and the following night it seemed as though the fountains of the deep were broken up. The next morning the rain ceased and the clouds cleared away, but the roads were so washed in many places as to be impassable and the streams were overflowing their banks, spreading devastation and ruin in every direction.

"Otter Creek rose to an unprecedented height, the waters overflowing the intervals to a vast extent on either side. When at the highest pitch they washed the door sills of the house of Stephen Mead on the west side, and boats were propelled on the line of the highway from Milton Potter's to Mr. Mead's. The bridge near Mrs. Cooley's as well as the Walker and Hammond bridges were swept away; but the Mead bridge was by great exertions saved, though its struc-

SWINGING BRIDGE ACROSS OTTER CREEK

ture was greatly damaged. When it was perceived that this was seriously endangered the neighboring inhabitants turned out and having taken up the planks piled heavy timbers on the rails so that the superincumbent weight was sufficient to resist the force and uplifting power of the water.

"At a special meeting called on the 3rd of September the town voted to raise two cents on a dollar on the list of 1811, payable in grain the first of January, 1812, and two cents on a dollar on the list of 1812, payable in grain the first of January, 1813, to rebuild and repair the four large bridges in said town carried off by the late freshet and to defray other expenses. Voted that the selectmen with the addition of Adget Lathrop and Ashbel Lee be a committee to superintend the building and repairing of the bridges aforesaid."

In 1849 when the railroad nosed its way down through the valley there were eighteen houses in the village of Sutherland Falls. This is the testimony of Myron Warner, one of the oldest residents. Some of these homes have already been brought into the story. Nearly all of the new ones were born of the mill yards. Three of them were in the hollow north of the old Library (Municipal Memorial). Two stood on the ledge west of the building shop. South or southwest of the Sutherland Falls quarry were three more. Still farther south was the Hills Taylor house which is standing today across the railway track from the grist mill, and in the fork of the roads north of McGary's store was the Samuel Kelley or William Maynard place.

Samuel Kelley, prior to 1837, lived in a little cabin which was perched on the knoll opposite what is now the Erik Lundquist lot. This South Street house was not built by Kelley but by someone who settled there

at an earlier day. Possibly it should have been considered among the first settlements of the neighborhood.
Joseph Kelley of Brandon, a son of Samuel Kelley,
maintains that it was a log cabin; other old residents
are equally insistent that it was a product of the saw
mill. In any event it has long since faded away into
the hazy past. The roof collapsed in 1852 and no one
intervened to save it from ruin.

East of what is now the Vermont Marble Company's office and on the other side of the railway track
stood a small brick building which was used as a post
office as early as 1848. Undoubtedly this was Uncle
Sam's first agency in Sutherland Falls although no
postmaster was officially assigned to the post until 1855.

As for the industries of the town in those days, the
Sutherland saw mill was in ruins in 1840. It is supposed that the grist mill struggled on to a somewhat
later period. A little west of the saw mill stood a wool
carding factory, also a forge shop for the manufacture
of bar iron, picks and unwrought nails. Both these
later plants derived their power from a dam in the
Beaver Pond Brook. They were operated by a man
named Spud Leonard and everything, even the nails,
was hammered out by hand. A part of the iron used in
the shop was dug out of the hill north of the Humphrey
farm house. Another basis of supply was in Pittsford
and some of it was even drawn by team from Crown
Point, N. Y. Profits must have been rather meager,
particularly on the Crown Point output, for the finished
product had to be hauled back to Troy before it could
be marketed. It was but logical therefore that the
forge should go the way of the saw mill and that the
carding shop should finally close its doors.

At one time in the early forties there was a lime

kiln where the Company's office was destined to rise. Another concern had an outfit for the manufacture of potash. On the mountain east of the falls were pits for the burning of charcoal. At the cross roads in Pittsford near the school house was a tannery and shoe shop run by N. S. Warner, the father of Myron Warner. In

MARKER ON MENDON ROAD SHOWING LIMIT OF RUT-
LAND JAIL YARD IN 1840

1820 Robert Wright built the town's third distillery but even this was abandoned after a few years of activity. So it seems that while the pioneers around the falls tried their hands at a diversity of industries, nearly all of them ended in the debtor's court.

In those unelastic times men could be imprisoned for debt. In Book 14 of the Rutland Records it is set forth that the Jesse Paul farm was mortgaged to Francis Slason and that Paul, being unable to pay, was placed behind the bars in 1835. This is the way the judgment of the court was worded:

"You are commanded to take the body of the said Jesse Paul and him to commit to the keeper of the jail in Rutland."

This is not saying that he would be cast into a dungeon. Theoretically he would be a prisoner but in actual practice he might be let out within what were termed jail limits, thus giving him a chance to work and cancel the indebtedness.

The "jail limits" for Rutland were a series of marble posts which marked the town line between Rutland and Pittsford. Each post was about two feet long and four inches square with a letter "J" cut in the top. Prisoners were allowed their freedom so long as they kept within the posts. This gave them a six mile area in which to labor. If they overstepped, they were run down and placed in confinement.

One of these posts was discovered in 1915 by H. P. Powers and F. B. Kingsbury. It was still keeping guard on the steep hill east of Beaver Pond. The others in this vicinity have either been buried or carted away. One was set thirty or forty rods north of the Sutherland Falls quarry; another was near the west bank of the Otter. It seems a pity that more of them could not have been kept on display as reminders of that period in our development when debt-paying was regarded as an abiding duty.

As an example of the treachery of fortune it should perhaps be pointed out that Francis Slawson,

himself, was walking inside those posts within an in-
credibly short number of years. He had become interested in the marble business and been caught in financial undercurrents. He was then living in West Rutland. He assured the court that by continuing his
business at Sutherland Falls he could right himself.
He was given the chance and there within jail limits he
freed himself from his creditors and took his place again
among the respected classes.

The year 1849 was memorable for at least two
reasons; the discovery of gold in California and the
completion of the Rutland & Burlington railroad. To
the dwellers in the Otter Creek valley there was little
question as to which of these events was most epochal.
The gold was far away but the iron track was near and
it verified the existence of a world of commerce. It
offered as they fancied a new order in transportation
facilities.

Even in these days of mechanical genius, the creation of a railroad is an undertaking of recognized magnitude. Obviously it must have been more of a problem
in forty-nine when nearly everything was measured
in terms of hand labor. Truly it was a mighty effort
which brought the Rutland & Burlington road into
being.

The worst cut on the entire line was the rocky ledge
north of Sutherland Falls. And how was this con-
quered? Not by steam or compressed air but by actual
brawn. Stagings were raised on the rocks one above the
other and there gangs of men kept hammering with
long hand drills, incessantly, day after day, until the
required level had been reached. It would be interesting
to look into the books of that early railway corporation
and see how much time was allotted to that one cut,

THE HILLS-TAYLOR HOUSE, BUILT IN 1840
THE KELLY, OR MAYNARD HOUSE, BUILT ABOUT 1830
THE ORMSBEE HOUSE, BUILT ABOUT 1830

but those pages like the road itself have been handed
down from owner to owner until there must be little
left of them.

The last spike was driven home in the fall of forty-
nine and a train of cars rolled into Pittsford for the
first time on the 19th of October. It had crawled down
from Burlington and for some unexplained reason it
remained over night in Pittsford, laboring on to Rutland the next forenoon. Possibly they ran out of water
and were forced to fill the boiler from the river. Or
they may have been ahead of their schedule, although
if later experiences may be taken as a criterion this is
hardly possible. Whatever may have caused the over-
night halt there is no intimation that the passengers
were disgusted or that they objected to the sleeping
accommodations which the road afforded.

The engine which pulled the train bore the flaming
title of "Red Bird." Here again we are in a quandary
as to why a locomotive should be connected with so
fanciful a name. It may be that in the last days of construction the painters were out of everything but red
and that the officials were thus compelled to bring
that color into the name. Surely the word "bird"
could not have been adopted as an augury of latent
ease of motion or speed.

In September, 1915, the Rutland News published
an interview with Daniel Austin, one of the town's
oldest men. Among other things it gives a colorful
picture of the outstanding achievement of 1849.

"The Rutland & Burlington railroad was completed as far north as Burlington and to celebrate that
event the road offered a free ride to anyone who wished
to visit the terminal. Mr. Austin took advantage of
the privilege to spend some time with his people

there. The occasion was a great one, and great were the 'doings' in the village of Burlington when the first visitors arrived by rail. Every tavern, boarding house and private house were filled and Mr. Austin and his party were obliged to drive to Winooski in order to find beds on the night of their arrival. Gatherings with speeches and fireworks marked the passing of the stage."

At the outset the service was usually limited to one train a day. Sutherland Falls was only a flag station and had little more than a platform on which to send off and receive its passengers. Mike Eagan was the first agent of the railroad company to take out a residence in Sutherland Falls, if indeed the little shanty in which he dwelt may be granted any such title. It was situated on the river side of the railway track north-east of the Old Library Building (Municipal Memorial). It is the judgment of those who are more or less in touch with the early traditions of the town that Mike Eagan was one of the real characters of his period.

In reality that first locomotive which steamed into Sutherland Falls was not a Red Bird at all. It was a Blue Bird, a symbol of happiness, the happiness which comes through anticipated prosperity. That was how it looked to the industrial pioneers on the day of its dedication. But with the passing of time these same pioneers were ready to swear that it had changed color. To them it was transformed into a Black Bird, an omen of gloom, simply because they had trusted too much to the railroad and had given too little consideration to the principles of organization and distribution on which modern industry has been founded. For twenty-five years after that gala day in 1849 the business interests at Sutherland Falls were in a state of perpetual uncertainty. There were many dreams but few realities—a few partial successes and more failures.

Looking at this period from another angle, while it may have been somewhat barren from an industrial viewpoint, it was considerably more productive as an experiment in social betterment. The inhabitants of the valley, especially those who had congregated around the Falls in answer to the siren calls of the short-lived mills and shops, were broadening into a more presentable community. They were casting off the habits of the wilderness and working back again to the ways of civilization. Moreover, they were in-augurating certain customs which had been impossible when the houses were scattered and out of touch with one another.

In 1870 the town of Rutland celebrated its one hundredth anniversary. Speaking at that time the Rev. John Todd drew this parallel between the old and what was then the new:

"Go back a century," he declared. "when the white man plunged tremblingly into the forest and came to the spot where the beautiful town now stands. His first object is to find a spring of water—near which he is to erect his little log cabin. There are no roads but the trail of the Indian. There are no neighbors—no forests yet cut down, no fields sown, no mills to grind his food or saw his lumber; no trading post where he may relieve a want; no physician when he is sick; no school for his child; no property by which he can supply his necessities. His music is the ring of the axe, and the falling of the trees. The night is made more solitary by the hooting of the owl and the scream of the wild beast. When he buries his dead he himself must make the coffin, dig the grave, and without a bell to toll, or a minister to offer a prayer, he must bury the dead under a tall tree. The pioneer must struggle with poverty, take nature in the rough, let sunshine into his house and heart by his own industry and struggles. His food is the plainest, his dress is the simplest, his home is the most humble, and the only thing that cheers him is a hope that his children will reap the benefit of all this self-denial.

"Go there a century after this. That beginning has become a mighty power. The same old mountains lift themselves up there but the forests are gone, the pleasant roads and bridges are all built, and a town, growing, thriving, prosperous, is there. The fields are under high culture, the meadows glow with promise and the town sits like a queen crowned with a wealth of beauty."

Allowing the venerable doctor a reasonable latitude for his happy allusion to the glamor and prosperity of 1870, his no doubt is a fair portrayal of the two widely divergent extremes. Even though none of the towns of that period were as exalted or advanced as their fathers believed them to be, they were at least getting started. They had their heads out of the wilderness and their faces set toward the light.

That at best was all that could be accredited to Sutherland Falls. It had done nothing memorable but it was freeing its feet from the underbrush and waiting for the opportune moment.

CHAPTER IV

SUTHERLAND FALLS IN THE SIXTIES

I N an old atlas published in 1869 there is a map which is supposed to represent the building development of Sutherland Falls up to that time. By tracing on that map the boundary lines of Proctor as they stand today it is comparatively easy to outline the growth of the community for another twenty-year period. Not the growth in wealth but a casual survey of the new roofs and something of what has taken place beneath the old ones.

Beginning at the northern outposts of the settlement, the Samuel Crippen property had passed into the control of Ransom Burditt. The clumsy cabin had faded away and in its place rested a frame structure. A few rods away was another house owned by Ransom Burditt which was rented by Austin Shangraw. Farther south at the fork of the roads was the Lewis White place, the same white house which Amos Crippen, the blacksmith, had conjured out of the uplands in 1814. Still farther south and down toward the river lived Eleazer Chapin Warner on what had once been called the David Crippen farm. Mr. Warner had purchased this estate in company with his father, Samuel Warner, and his brother, Nathan Smith Warner; then in 1841 he

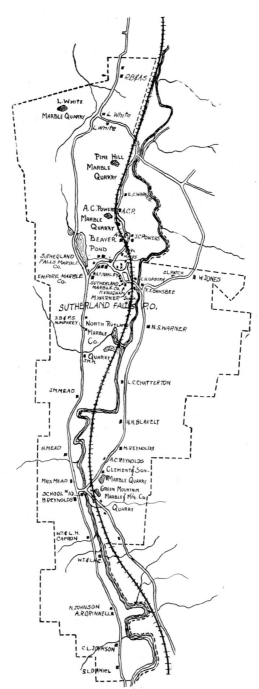

REPRODUCED FROM AN ATLAS MAP OF 1869, WITH DOTTED LINES
ADDED TO INDICATE PRESENT BOUNDARIES OF PROCTOR

had bought out their interests and become sole owner. The next house on the road to the Falls was that of Artemus C. Powers, the farm of James Ewing having descended to the sons of R. M. Powers, Artemus and Jeremiah. Five houses had sprung up on this land relinquished by Ewing, or possibly on land which had been added to the estate. Three were owned by A. C. Powers and two by his brother, J. C. Powers. The one farthest south was at the top of the hill on the western side of the road and the eminence which it crowned still upholds the title of "Powers' Hill."

Proceeding south on the West Road to Center Rutland, first came the Humphreys, David B. and Rawson S., living apparently in separate houses on the old ancestral estate. Then the Meads—Joel M. Mead on the section now operated by Will Mead, and Horatio Mead on what has since become known as the Stephen Mead place. A little south of the Double Roads Crossing was the Bradley Reynolds chimney. Next in order were the two Capron cabins, one of which has since been swept away by fire. The occupants at that time were W. T. and L. H. Capron, sons of Benjamin, the early settler. On the John Johnson domain several additional cellars had been walled and covered to meet the needs of the second generation. Nahum Johnson, the eldest son of John, was established in the old homestead. Cyrus, another son, had planted his hearthstone somewhat nearer Center Rutland. It was on the west side of the road not far from the entrance to Cummings Manor. Near the Nahum Johnson home was a small house built by A. R. Grinnell, his half brother, and a little farther away from the Cyrus Johnson place was the dwelling of I. L. Daniel.

Crossing over to the other side of the Creek, the

first building north of the Double Roads was under the proprietorship of I. C. Reynolds. This site is now approximated by the Vermont Marble Company's tenement which borders the west side of the road north of the Riverside quarry. On the east line of the high-way was the habitation of Morris Reynold, a property which under the Company's regime still wears the title of "Reynolds Farm." The house at the top of the hill, now designated the Dodge place, was tenanted by a brother-in-law of these two men, Brigham Proctor, who in turn passed it along to H. H. Blakely. Some would have it that these three Reynolds homes are standing today, that the old frames have simply been put through the ordinary crucible of repairing and remodeling. Be that as it may they show how the children of Morris Reynolds, senior, combined their efforts and worked the land on a cooperative plan. There were only two houses between the Blakely place and the Falls—the L. C. Chatterton stone fortress, later the town poor farm, and the N. S. Warner resi-dence which has since come into possession of Peter Morganson.

At the foot of Patch Hill were two other newcom-ers, J. L. Patch and William Jones. Mr. Patch moved to the Falls from Rutland in 1865. While living under the shadow of the hill he built the Ladabouche house which fronts the Proctor Memorial Library, and when that was completed he gave up the old for the new and transferred his furniture to the higher level. Thus originated the name "Patch Hill." Other incidents of his life will be set forth in the chapter on the marble industry.

The Patch farm house later became the home of William Manley and was finally moved away and con-

verted into two separate dwellings. The double tenement which today stands on the other side of the road
was made out of the old barn in which J. L. Patch
herded his stock. After the passing of the Patch estate
the land on which the buildings stood was lowered
fifteen feet, the sand being transferred by tramway to
the mills.

More or less mystery enshrouded the hut where
William or "Billy" Jones kept bachelor's hall. He was
charged by the gossips with being a deserter from the
British Army, but since the proof, if it existed at all,
was on the other side of the ocean, no one was disposed
to go after it. So he was allowed to go in and out without interference, and however he may have ignored
the call of the Army he seemed to have been unwaver-
ingly loyal to the call of the Falls. It is said that he
held the deed to five or six acres, kept two or three
cows, made his own butter, did his own cooking, and
that he was quite an efficient housekeeper, maintaining
an order within his shack which was utterly at variance
with what might have been expected of him. Tradition
persisted in whispering that he was the descendant of
a rich Irish family whose ancestral castle was not far
from Dublin. That part of his biography however
never grew into anything stronger than a whisper.

It would be unfair to a dawning industry, even
though that part of the story has been reserved for
other pages, to pass over this atlas map of sixty-nine
without pointing out some of the quarry holes which
had broken out in the valley. North of Beaver Pond
were the Shangraw or Mountain Dark and the Pine
Hill openings. To the south were the North Rutland,
or Columbian, near the Humphreys, and the Clement
and Son, and the Green Mountain across the road and

LOOKING SOUTH FROM TERRACE HILL, 1885

slightly to the south from what is now known as the Riverside quarry. Then there was the Sutherland Falls quarry within reach of the Falls, where through a strange twist of nature the blocks and the sawing power had been so faultlessly linked together.

This marble working activity was bringing men to the Falls who would not otherwise have come. In number of buildings the village was but little richer than in the days of forty-nine, but the names were changed, and almost without exception they were names connected in some way with the marble business. T. J. Ormsbee, whose cottage has since been replaced by the library; C. H. Osborn who lived where Senator Proctor was to rear his home; Fayette Vaughan; A. F. Manley; S. M. Dorr; J. J. Myers; all of these workers were given a place on the old atlas map and back of them like eternal question marks were ranged the Sutherland Falls Marble Co., the Empire Marble Co., Dorr & Myers and others of their kind. The question was: would they be able to fight their respective ways out of the gloom of uncertainty up to a stable profitable basis? But this belongs in the following chapter. It has simply thrust itself in at this point because of its eagerness to get into the story.

Looking over the town in this rather cursory fashion, one fact stands out above all others. At almost every point where a home was started in the early days of the wilderness it was still being maintained in 1869. Usually it was being kept alive by descendants of the pioneers—sometimes by other hands—but whatever the agency it was being guarded and expanded in preparation for the larger demands of the future. It was just this spirit of dogged persistency which converted the valley of the Otter into a livable country, clearing

LOOKING SOUTH FROM TERRACE HILL, 1890

away the fog and the marshes so that opportunity might not get lost in the mist.

A few buildings were blotted out during the period but this may have been due to the barrenness of the surroundings rather than to any fickleness of intention. The first cabins raised by R. M. Powers and Roger Stevens were in decay, likewise the Benjamin McIntire house, although the latter loss had been wrought by fire. And the roof of the Samuel Kelly place was half way to the cellar. With these few fatalities, and the possible addition of the Tuttle home, none of the old buildings had been permitted to fall into untimely or unmarked graves.

The Tuttle place was last occupied by an old her-mit named Benjamin Gould. It had reached the stage where no one else wanted it, and Gould undoubtedly was allowed to do as he pleased with it. Unlike Billy Jones his methods of housekeeping were not of the spotless variety, and if you ask any old resident about the conditions inside the Gould hut, it will invariably evoke a shrug of the shoulders or some other expression of disgust. It may be assumed therefore that Mr. Gould's reputation in the community was not of the best.

His chief claim to distinction rested on his building activities, or rather on a single constructive achieve-ment. It seems that as time went on the Tuttle house grew so decrepit and full of holes that even Gould con-sidered it unfit as a residence, and so he raised a hut of his own. It was on the extreme border of the Ormsbee land or, to speak in modern terms, on Hospital Hill in the neighborhood of the Churchill house. There was nothing miraculous about the shack except that it went up with Alladin-like celerity. It was built in a

LOOKING SOUTH FROM TERRACE HILL, 1922

day, so they say, complete from foundation to saddle-boards, and furthermore the owner has been credited with the statement that in two days he could have produced as good a house as anyone might wish to see. This feat, as compared with the ready-made walls and partitions of the present, looks less arduous than it really was.

It must not be forgotten that during the years which this chapter is supposed to chronicle the nation was thrust into a great conflict. And in Sutherland Falls, as in every other corner of Uncle Sam's dominion, men were infuriated and antagonized by the great god of war. The Old Library Building has opened its doors to more than one war meeting, and witnessed many sacred pledges of loyalty and sacrifice.

Several men enlisted from the Proctor section and went out with the first division in 1861. M. C. Warner, Willard S. Humphrey, Scott Maynard, Francis Ladabouche, Martin Brunson, Charles Stiles, Joseph White, Henry E. Wood—all these and perhaps more were really the representatives of Sutherland Falls, although some of their names appear on the roster of other towns. Mr. Warner was mustered in at Burlington. Brunson joined the sharp-shooters and afterward became a lieutenant. Both Warner and Stiles went first to Salisbury, where they enlisted in what was then known as the New England Cavalry. Later, after it had been decided to organize a Vermont regiment, the men were transferred to the Green Mountain Division. Nearly all the volunteers from the Falls were in the Second Vermont Battery.

It is inconceivable to picture a man of those days as lacking proficiency in the handling of firearms, but it seems that whatever else they may have attained

Camp Advance Sep. 28 1861

His Excellency Erastus Fairbanks
    Governor of Vermont
        Dear Sir

                Your favor of the 25th inst
tendering me the appointment of Major in the 5th Vt Regiment
is recd.

        With a due sense of the responsibility of the position
and of my own unfitness for it, but hoping to be guided
and sustained by a higher than earthly power, I accept
the position.

Thanking you for the appointment and for the very kind
terms in which you were pleased to offer it, I await your
orders to report to the Colonel of the Regiment

                Very Respectfy Your obt Servt
                    Redfield Proctor

LETTER WRITTEN BY REDFIELD PROCTOR, ACCEPTING COMMISSION
IN 5TH VERMONT REGIMENT

they were free from the taint of over-confidence. Mr. Warner relates that he and Stiles often met on the level ground at the base of Patch Hill for an hour or more of target practice. The target was placed near a little knoll. If it were standing today it would be in the way of the Greek Church. It had a nine-inch bullseye and the men stood eighty rods away.

Many other men, whose lives have been interwoven in varying degrees with the story of Proctor, gave unstintedly of their service to the cause of the Union. But they were not here when the call was sounded; they are the later arrivals in the valley. As in the case of other industrial centers, the population is subject to many changes. Veterans have come and gone. Some have set out from here on the last great journey. A few of the names will be recorded on subsequent pages, but by far the greater number must be dismissed with a word of fervent tribute.

Among the photographs which carry us back to the fighting days is one which reproduces a frayed and faded letter. This letter was written at Camp Advance, Sept. 28, 1861, and addressed to Erastus Fairbanks, Governor of Vermont. It reads as follows:

"Your favor of the 25 inst. tendering me the appointment of Major in the 5th Vermont Regiment is rec'd.

"With a deep sense of responsibility of the position and of my own unfitness for it, but hoping to be guided and sustained by higher than earthly power, I accept the position.

"Thanking you for the appointment and for the very kind terms in which you were pleased to offer it, I wait your orders to report to the Colonel of the Regiment."   Very Res'p'y your Ob't Servant,
REDFIELD PROCTOR.

ORMSBEE AVENUE

There is more in this letter than simply the accept-ance of a commission in the army. There is an index of those qualities of humility, directness and fortitude which were so richly dominant in the later life of Sena-tor Proctor, the qualities which made of him a valued officer in the service of his country and an industrial pioneer of the highest type. It would be unjust to the man and the town to hurry over this period without bringing in this little incident. Of all the participants in the mighty struggle, none has a better right to be identified with the Sutherland Falls honor roll.

Immediately preceding the war several buildings had been added to the village. Joseph Kelley, who was born in the cabin across the road from the Erik Lund-quist place, was one of the contractors of that period. With another man to help him he raised the Senator Proctor barn and did some work on the house. He also built the Benson cottage, bounded today on the north by the Company's stables and on the south by the Hartnitt property. All this work was done in the fifties. Mr. Kelly moved away from town in 1859.

In the Laws of Vermont for 1857 is "An Act In-corporating the Sutherland Falls Hotel Company." The incorporators were E. M. Madden, H. P. Roberts, E. P. Wheeler, W. S. Corwin, John M. Goodenough, A. C. Powers, E. L. Ormsbee, John Cain, and F. A. Fisher. They were authorized to hold property not in excess of forty thousand dollars and to erect a hotel and house of public entertainment at Sutherland Falls in the Town of Rutland.

No one of today can understand what the Falls people of 1855 could do with a forty-thousand-dollar hotel, nor is there any intimation as to where they proposed to erect it. In the fifties, when labor was cheap and timber was cheaper, an impressive showing might have been made with that amount of money, a creation which all the valley would envy. But alas, for plans! The war came on and the hotel died where it was born, in the halls of the legislature.

It was inevitable that life at the Falls should remain dormant throughout the war. Nothing attempted to grow in those harrowing days; if it did little came of the effort except reverses and regrets. The most that any community hoped to do was to keep its organization from being disrupted and completely overturned. Everybody was looking forward to the time when the ammunition money could be turned back again to civil life.

Toward the latter part of the war, the industrial tension at the Falls became somewhat less acute. A new manager was installed at the marble works and he promised many things. Indeed his promises were so varied and so visionary that they eventually led him into serious financial straits. But while they were being made, they seemed to be exactly what was needed to set the tottering business on its feet.

No, the end of the war was not the beginning of prosperity for Sutherland Falls. Between that and stability lay the depression and uncertainty of a receivership. Out of that receiver's court, however, emerged a leader, and with him the town and its marble rose to a position of permanence and nation-wide recognition.

CHAPTER V

RISE OF VERMONT MARBLE INDUSTRY

THE FIRST QUARRY—HUMPHREY'S MANUSCRIP
HISTORICAL ADDRESS—REMINISCENCES OF
OLD RESIDENTS—PRESENT DAY FACTS
AND FIGURES

IN a letter sent out in January, 1792, from Nathaniel Chipman of Rutland to Gen. Philip Schuyler o New York, there is a reference to the marble in terests of Vermont. So far as is known this is t he earlies written allusion to this branch of the state's resources

The letter referred to a conversation of the previous winter and went on to name over some of the products which might go to support a proposed canal between the Hudson River and Lake Champlain.

"There are also," he wrote, "in this part of the country numerous quarries of marble, some of them of superior quality. Machines may easily be erected for sawing it into slabs by water and in that state it might become an important article of commerce."

It is quite generally conceded that the first marble quarried in Vermont came from the town of Dorset. In a little booklet issued by the Middlebury Historical Society, we are told that Isaac Underhill opened a quarry there in 1785 and that the marble was first sold "for fire-jambs, chimney backs, hearths and lintels for the capacious fireplaces of the day." This at first may sound like a conflicting statement, since there are any number of old cemeteries in Vermont which contain native marble slabs erected in Revolutionary days. There is little liklihood, however, that those stones were taken from any quarry; they were doubtless split from the outstanding ledges; indeed they bear evidence of having been hammered into form in the crudest possible way.

So it is entirely within reason to attribute the first marble quarry to Dorset—not alone the first in Vermont, but in the entire Northern Continent. Pittsford claims to have begun quarrying operations in 1795, and the True-Blue quarry in West Rutland was probably one of the pioneers. But none of these contenders has ever been able to crowd out of first place the Dorset opening at the foot of Mt. Aeolus.

That the people of the state were early interested in the production of marble and its future prosperity is unmistakably set forth in the public records of 1832. The General Assembly of that year passed a resolution exhorting the Representatives in Congress "to use all honorable means to procure the passage of a law which shall effectaully protect our citizens engaged in the manufacture of marble from foreign competition."

In Mason's History of Rutland County is the digest of a manuscript left by R. S. Humphrey, one of the Proctor pioneers, a sketch of whose life has already been woven into this little book. Mr. Humphrey lived within sight of the original quarries; therefore his observations should be accurate as to detail. This in itself is sufficient excuse for reprinting the article.

He states, upon the authority of Samuel Butler, that the first marble taken from what was first known as the Humphrey quarry, afterward owned by the Columbian Marble Company, was in the fall of the

year 1836, and that the first saw started at the falls
for sawing marble was on Monday, the 26th day of
September, 1837.

"In the summer of 1836 Willard and Moses Humphrey became convinced that the quarrying and sawing
of marble could be made profiable. They had little
capital; there were no railroads; there was no postoffice nearer than Pittsford and West Rutland; and
they were entirely lacking in practical knowledge of
the work they resolved to undertake. The first work
was done in the Columbian Quarry by blasting out
the blocks with gunpowder, hauling them with ropes,
pulleys and rollers up an inclined plane to a wagon or
sled, and thence to the falls with oxen. Several small
openings were made in prospecting for marble, one of
which was about thirty rods north of the first or Columbian opening, one on the Capron Farm, and one west
of the Capron house, near the back road. But they did
not begin work on what was afterward distinguished
as the Sutherland Falls Quarry until the summer of
1838. The building of the first mill, with four gangs of
saws, was begun in the winter of 1836-37, previous to
which date they had associated with themselves Edgar
L. Ormsbee, of Rutland, under the firm name of Humphrey & Ormsbee. On the 26th day of September,
1837, the first saws began to swing. Up to this time
not more than five or six men had ever been employed
by the firm at one time. The mill was a substantial
stone building, part of the walls of which helped to
form the north wall of the 'Lower Mill.'

"The financial crises of 1837-38 crushed all business
at this point, and after a struggle of about a year from
the time when sawing began, the firm yielded to the
pressure, gave up everything to their creditors and

SUTHERLAND FALLS MARBLE COMPANY'S FIRST MILL.

assigned to Francis Slason of West Rutland. Under his
direction the business was carried on three or four years,
with Moses Humphrey as superintendent. The Humphrey Brothers soon gave up all interest in the business
and removed from the place. Mr. Ormsbee retained
some hold upon the property and associated himself
with his brother, Thomas J. Ormsbee, who carried on
the business two years longer. Their principal business
was sawing marble that was drawn there from West
Rutland, the local trade taking most of the sawed
stock, and a small part of it finding its way via Whitehall to points farther west. Between 1845 and 1854 the
marble business at Sutherland Falls was substantially
at a stand-still, quarries having in the mean time been
opened at West and Center Rutland, and larger mills
erected. The woodwork in the old mill fell into decay,
the quarry openings became frog ponds, and the entire
enterprise seemed to have dropped into permanent
stagnation.

"For a few years before his death in 1848 Joseph
Humphrey, Jr., had carried on a business of considerable importance for the time in finishing grave-stones
in a shop built by himself. A part of the period he was
associated with Hills Taylor, under the firm name of
Humphrey & Taylor, and their work attained a favorable local reputation.

"In the year 1854 the North River Mining Company,
which had been prospecting for marble in the town of
Sudbury, undertook the resuscitation of the Sutherland
Falls business. The railroad was now in operation,
supplying means of transportation, and circumstances
seemed more favorable for the business. But the quarries at West Rutland had been largely worked, as we
have before shown, and there was a large quantity of

SUTHERLAND FALLS MARBLE COMPANY'S YARD IN 1868

the marble in the market. In fact the active competition inspired by the energetic men of West Rutland made it difficult to market the Sutherland Falls marble in large quantities. The old mill had been rebuilt and started, however, and some of the Sudbury marble sawed. A small business was started and it gradually grew, one of the favorable conditions being the excellence of the marble of this locality for out-door uses. But the slow growth of the trade and other causes told heavily upon the resources of the Company, and in 1857, after a three years' struggle, the Company failed. All business was again suspended.

"The management of the works during this Company's regime was in the hands of Francis A. Fisher, who resided at the Falls until 1866, when he removed to Rutland, and lived there until his death, which occurred in 1878. Older residents will remember Mr. Fisher as the father of Mrs. John N. Woodfin.

"In 1857 a reorganization was effected and the 'Sutherland Falls Marble Company' was formed. It contained as its leading spirits such men as George Madden of Middletown, N. Y.; Emerson Bryant of Boston; Ex-Governor John B. Page; and Judge John Prout of Rutland; H. P. Roberts assumed the position of Superintendent and Manager. The business now began to grow. A few more houses for workmen were erected and six gangs of saws were added to the mill. The real merits and beauties of the marble combined to foster the steady growth of the business at this point and it prospered accordingly.

"Mr. Roberts, the Manager, lived at the Falls five or six years and was succeeded by J. S. Hughes of Middletown, N. Y. Both of these men became engaged in railroad contracting after leaving this place.

SUTHERLAND FALLS MARBLE COMPANY'S YARD IN 1878

A. C. Wicker, of Fair Haven, was bookkeeper and clerk for a short period, and after his departure Warren Decker assumed the position. Between 1860 and 1864 J. E. Corwin was clerk for about two years. He became in later years a bank president in Indiana. Mr. Humphrey mentions among those whose faces were familiar at the time of which we are writing, either in connection with the marble industry or otherwise about the place, A. F. Manley, who was foreman for years of the quarry, Hills Taylor, who worked many years in the Coping Shop, William Maynard, Henry and G. J. Cady, James and David Rogers, J. C. and A. C. Powers, William and D. B. Humphrey, N. S. Warner, Leverett Chatterton and others.

"In the year 1864 J. B. Reynolds became General Superintendent and Manager of the marble business at the Falls. Under his administration the industry made material advancement. The mill was increased to twelve gangs, tenement houses erected, etc. It is claimed, also, that some of the investments, particularly for the 'Crane Shed,' with machinery for handling and storing marble, that cost about $40,000, and the project of carrying water in a penstock from Beaver Pond for propelling the hoisting machine and pumping the quarry, with other extensive operations, were unwise and resulted in heavy loss. Harvey Reynolds, a brother of the Superintendent, was interested in the business for a time, and in connection with A. F. Manley had a contract for quarrying marble by the foot.

"J. B. Reynolds finally made a contract with S M.. Dorr and J. J. Myers by which they were to carry on the business of sawing and selling the marble under a lease. While this arrangement was in force Dorr &

Myers purchased of T. J. Ormsbee the land and water
privileges where the present large mill stands, and in
1867-68 they erected the first eight-gang mill on the
site. It was their enterprise, also, that first conveyed
the motive power from the water-way at the level of
the old mill in the hollow, up to the level of the railroad track, where the bulk of the great business is now
done.

"The business as conducted by Dorr & Myers,
through some complications and differences which
need not be detailed, was finally placed in the hands
of a receiver, in the person of Redfield Proctor. He
assumed the management of the interest in the fall of
1869 and removed to Sutherland Falls, April 15, 1871."

Speaking before the salesmen and department heads
at the Proctor Conference of 1920, Mr. Partridge told
something of the beginning and more of the vicissitudes
and ailments which beset the newly-christened Vermont Marble Company. He also sketched the growth
of the industry up to the fulness of the present day.
There can be no more efficient method of telling the
story than to quote his talk in full, enlarging afterward
on such phases of it as may have a local interest and
adding certain items which have been acquired from
other sources.

The address was as follows:

The original sign on our present main office at Proctor,
built in 1886, bore these figures, "1836-1886," a spread of a
half century. The first marble quarried in Sutherland Falls,
now Proctor, was in 1836 and the original pioneers were
Willard and Moses Humphrey, with whom was associated
Edgar L. Ormsbee, a lawyer of Rutland. They built the
first mill of four gangs in 1837. It was a part of the old lower
mill near the water power intake from the Creek, now long

since dismantled and its site covered by a marble fill reaching above the original top of the mill. The first quarrying is supposed to have been done at the Columbian quarry near the Humphrey homestead and quarrying at or near the old Sutherland Falls quarry probably began in 1838. The enterprise was carried on for three or four years and then fell into financial trouble. It resulted in the moving to Proctor in 1843 of Thomas J. Ormsbee, brother of Edgar L. Ormsbee, and he conducted the business for a couple of years more. Thomas J. Ormsbee continued to live at Proctor until his death in 1896 on the site now occupied by the public library. The bronze tablet on the boulder opposite the library well says that he and his wife "were active in all good works."

Between 1845 and 1854 the business was at a standstill. In the latter year the North River Mining Company, which had been doing some marble prospecting at Sudbury, took up the business at Proctor, but they failed in 1857. Then the first Sutherland Falls Marble Company was formed by gentlemen in Rutland, including John B. Page, afterwards governor, John Prout, afterwards judge of the Supreme Court, John B. Reynolds and others. At this time six gangs were added to the old lower mill.

About 1867 the Sutherland Falls Marble Company contracted with Dorr and Myers to saw some of their marble. Dorr and Myers purchased land and water privileges from Thomas J. Ormsbee and erected an eight-gang mill, which is now the first story of the eight-gang mill in the present line of mills. Dorr and Myers were both sons-in-law of William Y. Ripley, whose name will later appear in the development of the Rutland deposit. Mrs. Dorr was the well-known author, Julia C. R. Dorr. In 1869 Dorr and Myers, having some business differences, sought in the courts a dissolution of their partnership and it resulted in the appointment of Colonel Redfield Proctor as receiver. Thus began the first connection of Colonel Proctor with the marble business in November, 1869.

At that time the business of Dorr and Myers consisted simply of their eight-gang mill and the rest of the marble business at Proctor was owned by the Sutherland Falls Marble Co., a Massachusetts corporation, operating the quarry

SUTHERLAND FALLS QUARRY 1885

FIRST MARBLE CHANNELING MACHINE, USED IN SUTHERLAND FALLS
QUARRY UNTIL ABOUT 1868

and ten gangs. Colonel Proctor no sooner came into touch
with the business here than he had a vision. Here were a
wonderful water power, capable of great development, a
promising quarry, a good deposit of sand on the site of the
present marble yard and the railroad immediately at hand.
He apparently early decided that, if he could bring together
the property into one ownership, it afforded under efficient
and economical management an excellent basis for a prosperous business. He therefore organized, in November, 1870,
the Sutherland Falls Marble Company, a Vermont corporation, which took over the whole, and in that new venture he
invested all that he had and all that he could borrow and became its treasurer and resident manager.

The next ten years from 1870 to 1880 were truly pioneer
days. Everything was upon a relatively small and simple
basis. Colonel Proctor often handled a truck and helped to
load cars, emphasizing the fact that the way to get returns
is to get off marble. He personally selected marble and it
was he who taught Mr. Taylor, the dean of our marble expert
department, how to select marble. During these years Colonel Proctor devoted himself night and day to the building up
of the business. To the best of my belief in all those years
the company never paid any dividends. What it could earn
was put into paying debts and extending the business. The
old Sutherland Falls quarry proved to be a great success and
in a way it was the foundation upon which the whole structure
of the Vermont Marble Company was eventually reared.
In 1880 at the end of ten years the Sutherland Falls Marble
Company was operating 64 gangs and had become a con-
spicuous success in the marble business of Vermont.

*   *   *   *   *   *

At West Rutland marble is supposed to have been taken
out at or near the True Blue quarry as early as 1807 and the
old Standard quarry to have been begun in the '30s. The
opening of the West Rutland marble deposit proper did
not begin until 1844. In that and the following year Mr.
Barnes began an opening on the property which subsequently became the property of the Rutland Marble Company;

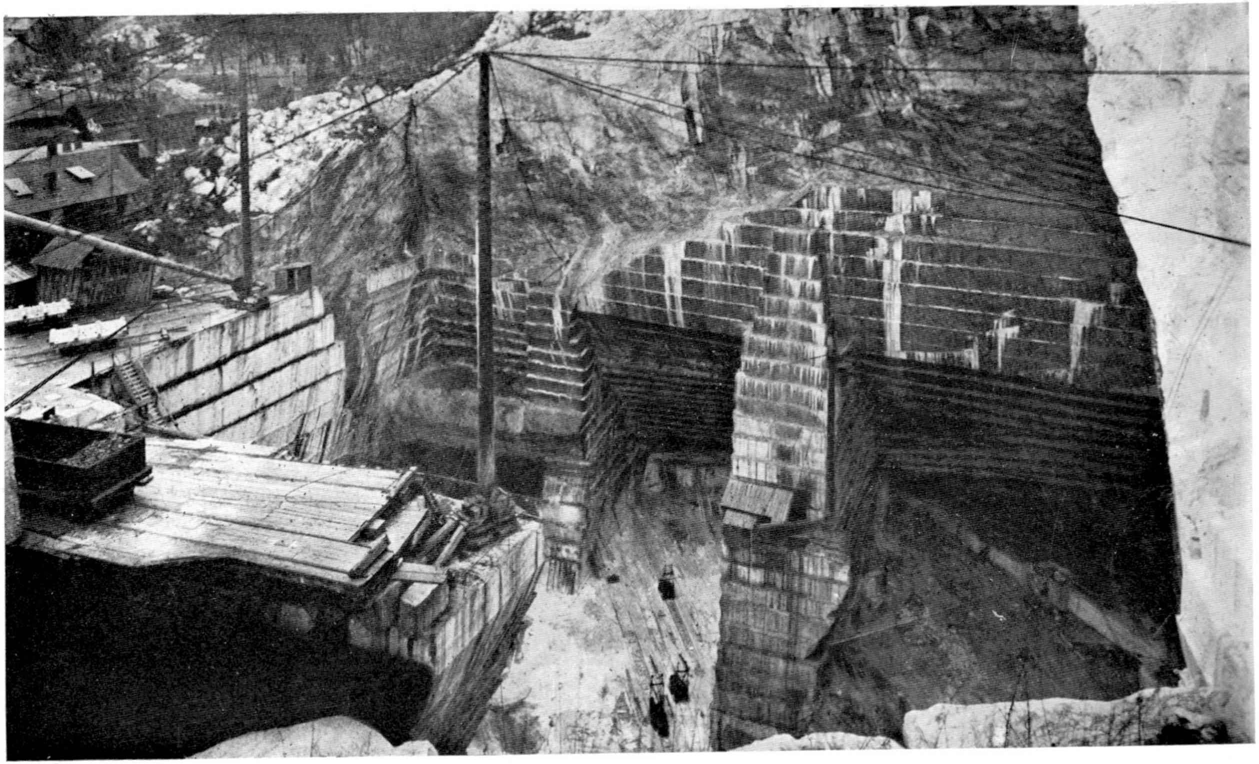

SUTHERLAND FALLS QUARRY, 1905

Mr. Sheldon an opening on the property of Sheldon & Sons; and Adams and Allen on the property which subsequently became the quarry of Gilson & Woodfin. Mr. Barnes was a retired minister. He had the faith necessary for the starting of a new enterprise but like many pioneers his lack of other qualities or the inopportuneness of the times did not permit him to reap its substantial rewards. After a varied fortune he finally met his death by a small piece of rock falling from the top of the quarry and striking him upon the head. Mr. Barnes early associated with himself William Y. Ripley, the father of General William Y. W. Ripley and General Edward H. Ripley, who later constituted the firm of Ripley Sons. They built the Ripley mill at Center Rutland on the site of the present Ripley mill, but eventually divided their properties, Ripley taking the mill at Center Rutland and Barnes the quarries at West Rutland, subject to a contract, however, to supply forever a specified number of cubic feet of marble which Ripley was to saw and sell and then divide the proceeds as he made collections.

One of the first men to make some measure of success with the Barnes properties at West Rutland was General Baxter, who at the beginning of the Civil War was Adjutant General of the state. General Baxter continued in the marble business for a few years and the Barnes properties then passed into the hands of the Rutland Marble Company, a New York corporation, largely owned by bankers and financiers in New York City.

At Center Rutland, besides the Ripley mill, another marble mill was early built at the present Center Rutland site. Mr. Charles Clement became interested in the business there and a mill on the site of the present new mill at Center Rutland was for many years called the Clement mill. The property at Center Rutland, not including, however, he Ripley mill, also passed into the ownership of the Rutland Marble Company.

In 1880 the Rutland Marble Company had, besides its quarries at West Rutland, which covered the largest holding on the West Rutland deposit, 24 gangs at West Rutland, 28 gangs at Center Rutland, and 8 gangs at Salem, N. Y., a total of 60 gangs. The contrast in methods and policies be-

tween the Rutland Marble Company and the Sutherland
Falls Marble Company was very marked. At Sutherland
Falls there was no division of profits. All earnings were devoted to the upbuilding and expansion of the business. On
the other hand the Rutland Marble Company, owned largely
in a distant city, was operated on directly the opposite theory.
One practice pursued by it, which seems ludicrous now, was
to hold auctions at their yards in Vermont for the sale of
marble to the great demoralization of the trade generally.

*   *   *   *   *

At an early session of this conference Mr. Howard, our
first vice-president, with a flight of poetic imagination which
rather startled me, spoke of the marriage of the Sutherland
Falls quarry with the West Rutland deposit. Adopting his
figure you may be interested to know that it was a case of
love at first sight. In 1880 Colonel Proctor, who was then
governor of the state, was in the office of a friend in New
York City when Elisha Riggs, a New York banker and president of the Rutland Marble Company, came in. The friend
said to Mr. Riggs that he presumed he knew Governor Proctor and Mr. Riggs replied he never had had the pleasure of
meeting him but he knew all about him and had been thinking for some time that he would like to have a visit with him.
Mr. Riggs told Governor Proctor that he knew he was making a success of the Sutherland Falls Marble Company, that
he felt his company had a good property at West Rutland
but it was not succeeding. He asked Governor Proctor if he
would consent to assume the management of the Rutland
Marble Company, and, that he might have a free hand, he
proposed to resign and have Governor Proctor elected president of the Company. That was done that same day at a
hastily called meeting of the directors and Governor Proctor
returned to Vermont that night to walk into the office of his
chief competitor the next morning with the suggestion that
he would like to look over their books.

Governor Proctor was in charge of the Rutland Marble
Company only a few months before he had a second vision

and that was the usefulness to both of a union of the two
properties of which he thus found himself in charge. Thus
in September, 1880, he formed and became President of the
Vermont Marble Company, a New York corporation, which
took over the property of the Sutherland Falls Marble Company and the Rutland Marble Company. It was a bold and
courageous step to permit an independent successful business
free from debt in which he or his immediate friends owned a
controlling interest to be merged into a new company, with
a considerable debt and a part of its business theretofore
unsuccessful, in which he became a minority stockholder.
The wisdom of the union, however, has been wonderfully
fulfilled and both parts of the business have grown in a way
that neither alone could have done.

*   *   *   *   *

At this time competitive conditions were much demor-
alized, as you may imagine from the reference to the auctions
of the Rutland Marble Company. To meet this situation
Governor Proctor devised and procured the organization of
the so-called Producers Marble Company, January 1, 1883.
It was not a corporation but a partnership of its five members permitted by general legislation secured for the purpose
to do business and to sue and be sued by its common name.
The members of the Producers Marble Company ceased to
sell any marble direct to the trade, but sold their entire production to the Producers Marble Company, which resold to
the trade. All invoices went out in the name of the Producers Marble Company, all collections were made by it, and
all the branches and travelers were under its control. The
Producers Marble Company gave notes to the members
semi-monthly for the marble which they had furnished less
a wholesale discount. Whether such a sales company might
not now come under the condemnation of the much later
Sherman anti-trust act is a fair question, but it was not con-
trary to any law or business ethics then, and was perfectly
open and generally accepted by the trade as a useful instru-
ment for the distribution of Vermont marble and the stabilizing of its price. The proportion of the different partners

in the Producers Marble Company was Vermont Marble Company 54.72%, Sheldon & Sons 23%, Dorset Marble Company 8%, Ripley Sons 7.25%, Gilson & Woodfin 7.03%, and they were entitled to furnish marble through the Producers Marble Company as near as could be according to those per cents. The Producers Marble Company continued for five years, expiring by limitation December 31, 1887.

After the dissolution of the Producers Marble Company, Gilson & Woodfin joined with the Vermont Marble Company in the operation of branches and travelers during the year 1888. The other companies ran independently, except the Dorset Marble Company, which had gone into the hands of receivers before the expiration of the Producers Marble Company. Now followed in rapid succession the purchase by the Vermont Marble Company of the properties of the companies which had been its associates in the Producers Marble Company. January 1, 1889, it purchased from Gilson & Woodfin their entire property including the present so-called Gilson & Woodfin quarry and a mill upon a part of the site of the new mill now building at West Rutland.

Later in 1889 the mill of Ripley & Sons at Center Rutland was purchased. This added no quarry property as such to our holdings but did relieve the Vermont Marble Company from the vexatious requirements of the old Ripley-Barnes contract. That contract had always been a source of irritation between the parties in interest and at one time resulted in a suit between Ripley Sons and the Rutland Marble Company which went to the United States Supreme Court and was there argued by four of the most distinguished men at the bar of the United States at that time—Senator George F. Edmunds, long senator from Vermont, William M. Evarts, senator, secretary of state, etc., Edward J. Phelps, later ambassador to Great Britain, and B. R. Curtis. The opportunity to merge this contract was the larger motive for the Ripley purchase.

In 1891 the Sheldon purchase was effected. They had a considerable business and owned an excellent part of the deposit. The owners and managers were men liked in the trade and by their employes, but their financial management was unfortunate and their business accumulated gradually a larger and larger debt which they were unable to carry longer. We first connected ourselves with the property by making a lease of it for thirty years, but a little later purchased the capital stock of the Sheldon Marble Company and eventually it was merged into the Vermont Marble Company.

The so-called Sherman quarry at the north end of the West Rutland deposit during the time of the Producers belonged to the Dorset Marble Company. After the breakup of the Dorset Marble Company it passed into the hands of some gentlemen who had a mortgage on it, and it was purchased by us in 1891, thus completing our ownership of the great West Rutland deposit.

The Clarendon & Pittsford Railroad was begun north from Proctor in 1886 and to Center Rutland and West Rutland in 1887 and 1888, thus conveniently uniting the main properties.

*   *   *   *   *

The early marble business consisted of the sale of sawed marble for monumental uses. It was not until about 1876 that we began to do monumental finishing. About that time a small shop was started here at Proctor and the Vermont Marble Company began in 1880 with that shop and a small shop which the Rutland Marble Company had at Center Rutland. The monumental finishing business has grown gradually to its present large proportions.

Exterior finishing was begun in 1880. It first began in a small way with contractors coming here and cutting marble furnished by us. In the price list of the Sutherland Falls Marble Company dated May 1, 1880, the announcement was made that the company had engaged an experienced foreman from New York who would give his entire attention to our building work. That was Thomas J. Hagan, and for several years he was foreman of the shop, draftsman, salesman, etc., combined. It was not until 1884 that he even required a helper. Then Mr. James H. Edson, brother of our Assistant Treasurer, was transferred from the position of office boy at the Producers Marble Company office to become his assist-

OFFICE AND MILLS LOOKING NORTH IN 1885

ant in office and drafting work, and Mr. Edson after a few years succeeded Mr. Hagan as the head of the exterior department.

The first branch established by the Sutherland Falls Marble Company was at Toledo about 1875, and its first manager was Henry D. Pierce, now manager emeritus of the Chicago Branch. Mr. Pierce came from Senator Proctor's native town; he went into the army during the Civil war as a mere boy, afterwards he fitted for college, graduated at Dartmouth and became a teacher in the high school at Toledo. When Senator Proctor started the branch at Toledo he persuaded Mr. Pierce to give up his teaching to go into the marble business. About the same time or soon after the Sutherland Falls Marble Company started a branch in Boston and it had two branches in 1878. In January, 1881, after the organization of the Vermont Marble Company, we had four branches—Boston, Philadelphia, Toledo and Chicago. During the life of the Producers Marble Company there was a great increase in the number of branches. In 1883 there were nine and in 1886, eleven, including the branches at Cincinnati, Toledo, Detroit and Kansas City. With the dissolution of the Producers Marble Company some of these branches were given up and in 1891 the Vermont Marble Company had six branches only. Our oldest branch, therefore, is Boston and our next oldest are Philadelphia and Chicago.

In 1889 Redfield Proctor became secretary of war in the cabinet of President Harrison, and in 1891 United States Senator, in which office he continued until his death March 4, 1908. When he went to Washington in 1889 he resigned as president and director of the Company. Our treasurer, Mr. Morse, has the honor of being his successor on the board of directors. Senator Proctor immediately dropped all of the details of the business although he ever continued to be deeply interested in what it was doing. I have recounted the purchases in 1889 to 1891 and treated them as a part of his administration because they were largely initiated and fostered by him and I think properly belong there. In the public mind, however, his name was so connected with the success of the business that so long

OFFICE AND MILLS LOOKING NORTH IN 1893

as he lived he was accustomed to personally endorse the notes of the Company. It is a tribute to the public confidence in him that although banks knew or at least might have known that substantially all of the property he had was risked in the business, still the presence of his personal name upon the back of the company's notes made for their acceptability on the part of all discriminating bankers.

Senator Proctor, the founder of this business, was one of the most extraordinary men it has ever been my privilege to know. Of restless ambition, iron will, farseeing vision and abounding energy, he laid the foundations for the business, carried it through the years of its infancy and most strenuous trials, and after him it continued to grow along the lines which he laid down. He concentrated all his efforts in one particular line, refusing all allurements to other business fields. In the marble business itself he made investments which might have seemed reckless to those with less abounding faith, but he made no other business investments. It was by the application of these simple principles, concentration, energy, singleness of purpose, organization, economy, spending in the business all that it could earn, that under his master hand from so small beginnings grew so large results.

*   *   *   *   *

Fletcher D. Proctor succeeded his father as president in 1889 and continued as president until his decease September 27, 1911, a period of over twenty-two years. In 1889, or perhaps better in 1891, when the large purchases at West Rutland were concluded, there had been brought together interests which theretofore had been operated independently and quite diversely. The problem was how to consolidate the whole into a single unit and how to organize them upon a more systematic and businesslike basis. This was successfully done and during the next twenty-two years the company enjoyed a continuing growth and development. It was during this period that the company largely assumed its present form and organization.

Our interior building business did not begin until after

OFFICE AND MILLS LOOKING NORTH IN 1922

the panic of 1893. Incited by the dire need of more work to do we then began to develop the use of our marble for interior building purposes and gradually became able to devote to beautiful and artistic uses some marble which before had not been regarded as suitable for monuments and had been thrown away as waste. It was a great achievement and much credit for it is due to Mr. Howard and Mr. Higbee. Our non-monumental business—of which interior building was the larger part—came before the war to be fully sixty per cent of our business.

The electrification of the Sutherland Falls power was made in 1905 and 1906. Huntington Falls was bought and electrically developed in 1910. Beldens Falls, which we purchased in 1904, was electrically developed in 1913. These three great powers with other lesser ones are tied together with our various quarries and mills by seventy-three miles of high voltage line. Not being a public service corporation and having no right of eminent domain, we had to secure by contract with private owners rights of way for the pole line for the entire distance, a task accomplished with great success by Mr. Boyce, our superintendent of real estate.

We made our first investment in Alaska in 1908 and began the successful development which we have made there. This present year we have purchased two considerable properties in Alaska for the further strengthening and enlarging of our business there.

We first bought a controlling stock interest in the Barney Marble Company in 1901 and subsequently acquired its full ownership. This gave us the possession of the Verde Antique deposit at Roxbury and the Champlain marble deposits at Swanton and the plant at Swanton. The larger development and the wonderful success of Verde Antique has come since we began to operate at Roxbury.

The Albertson property was purchased in 1899 and the old mill afterwards replaced by the present crane mill. We began our purchases at Danby in 1905. In 1909 we acquired the property of the Brandon Italian Marble Company, giving us our present quarries at Brandon and the plant at Middlebury. The development of the West Blue,

commonly called the Harrington quarry, was begun in 1901.
In 1911, shortly before the decease of Fletcher D. Proctor,
we purchased the property of the Rutland Florence, including the Florence mill, the Pittsford Italian quarries and the
quarry and mill of the True Blue at West Rutland. This is
the largest single addition to our property since the Sheldon
purchase.

Governor Fletcher D. Proctor—he became governor of
our state in 1906—was a man of real administrative genius,
remarkable judgment of men, rare mastery of details and
a splendid organizer. The business which his father founded
he developed, enlarged and systematized upon an enduring
basis. He had a natural capacity for business and affairs,
and his wisdom and energy were a predominating element
in the business for twenty-two years. In close touch with
each department of the business and particularly the pro-
ducing end he had great capacity for coordinating the work
of all. Like his father, he had the happy faculty of commanding the respect, confidence and perfect loyalty of those who
were associated with him. Senator Proctor drew around
himself men much younger than himself, whose work he
guided and directed. Fletcher, being only 28 when he became
president, had perhaps the harder task of holding together
in perfect loyalty and understanding men nearer his own
age. Each had his own peculiar mission in the history of the
business and each was fitted for it. I cannot think of either
doing the task of the other with equal success.

*   *   *   *   *

The course of events since 1911 is too recent to require
any detailed comment, and is generally known to you. The
fact that the organization has worked smoothly and with
measurable success since then is a tribute to the way Governor Proctor left it. During four years of the time we were
in the midst of the Great War when the problem for the
marble business fixed by the course of events was one of
existence. We have, however, started our development at
San Saba and our branches at Dallas, Texas, and Peterboro,
Ontario. We have rounded out our holding at Danby and

Dorset through the purchase of the Norcross properties in 1913 and by large development work at Danby have put ourselves in a better position to handle building business in the future. During the last nine years some innovations have been introduced, because in the natural course of events the time had come when we could undertake them. Our accounting system has been much improved so that we know the results much more in detail, enabling us to conduct our business more closely. That information has brought us some surprises from which we are trying to profit. We have established our pension system and it is working very satisfactorily. We are today generally better organized and in a stronger position than we were nine years ago.

*   *   *   *   *

The Vermont Marble Company has thus grown through the years from small beginnings to become a large institution by the steady application of simple fundamental principles. During fifty years it has established itself as an institution with some definite policies which it is worth while to recall.

It has always pursued a system of sound finance, and has never engaged in frenzied finance nor attempted promotion schemes. Unfortunately it has been the innocent excuse for schemes of frenzied finance by others, for I suppose that every wildcat proposition for getting rich quickly in marble, which has been put out to bleed the public in recent years, has been based upon alluring and misleading statements of the remarkable success of the Vermont Marble Company. These promoters do not tell the public that our success was built upon long years of patient waiting, by the happy blending of natural opportunity, sustained effort and great self-sacrifice.

The management of the company has always given the enterprise fair treatment. It has not followed the false philosophy that one can eat his apple and still have it. Steadily year after year it devoted all that it earned to the enlargement of the property or the payment of debts. Its dividend policy was one of the most extreme conservatism I have ever known. As I have said to you, to the best of my belief the Sutherland Falls Marble Company from 1870 to 1880 paid no dividends whatever. From 1880 to June 1, 1901, when the company was reorganized on the Senator's seventieth birthday as a Vermont corporation, a period of twenty-one years, the company paid altogether only 13 per cent in dividends, an average of seven-tenths of one per cent per year. There are some simple mathematics very interesting in this connection. One dollar put at 6% compound interest for 21 years would become $3.40. If we assume, therefore, that the Vermont Marble Company in these years earned as much as 6.7% annually, which is too small a return for a precarious mining venture, thus saving 6% a year, the value of its property and assets should have been 3.4 times larger in 1901 than in 1880.

The policy of insurance from size and diversity has constantly been kept in mind. The ownership of one marble quarry is very precarious. The ownership of many marble quarries of diverse kinds and differently located may be fairly stable. The use of marble for one purpose only has in it many more contingencies than when used for very diversified purposes. It is similar to the principle of life insurance. The insurance of one life is too risky, the insurance of many makes a stable business. Much of the stability of the Vermont Marble Company has been gained by the size and diversity of its holdings and undertakings.

Perhaps the greatest asset of the company, and it is the result of a historical policy, is its loyal organization. It comes in some degree at least from the close association of all those who are associated together in the business. One of the most significant events in the history of the Vermont Marble Company is when Senator Proctor, April 15th, 1871, moved his family to this village, which subsequently came to bear his name. In that event and in the adherence to that example of his family and of others associated in the management was laid the foundation of the best kind of relation. As I have said before, "Many of the misunderstandings which arise between large corporations and their employes are due to the fact that such corporations are more often owned and in a larger sense managed by absentees. If the local managers are not the controlling owners, but are held accountable for certain financial results by a board of directors sitting in some distant city, neighborly considerations do not have a fair chance. One of the unavoidable, but none the less unfortunate, incidents of great corporate enterprises is that they so often prevent employers and employes from living in personal touch with each other as neighbors in the same community." Upon that foundation and upon the foundation of mutual trust and confidence there has grown up one of the most loyal organizations which any large business has.

The Vermont Marble Company has striven to give of the stability which it has built up for itself as largely as possible to its employes. It has been its policy to give to its employes as steady employment as possible, the business as a whole carrying the contingencies of business rather than, as is so often done, to lay off and to take on its employes according to variations in trade.

It has always been the policy of the company to keep itself in direct contact with the trade. This it has done through its system of branches and agents who cover the entire field. Through it and through the quality of service which we have been able to render the company has built up another great asset, the good-will of the trade. We do not carry it on our books, as some companies do, expressed in dollars and cents, but it is one of our most valuable assets.

Thus the Vermont Marble Company under wise leadership, by faithful adherence to very simple economical principles, has become much the largest marble company in the world. Its largest possessions are not physical properties but wise policies and intangible assets to which I have referred. It is a great inheritance which has been committed to us.

Going back to the beginning once more, that little old mill in which the Humphrey brothers sawed their first marble, was a low gable-roof structure, which was said to stand on the exact site of John Sutherland's Grist Mill. It was later reinforced by a stone addition on the north and one of wood on the south. The latter addition, known as the "Air Compressor Building," was raised in 1877. It was equipped by machines which had been used in the construction of the Hoosic Tunnel, and a pipe was laid to the Sutherland Falls opening so that the air could be transferred from the room in the hollow and made to run the drills in the quarry.

Albert F. Manley was the first foreman of the Sutherland Falls Quarry. Among the laborers were William Ward, Jeff Howard, Moses Humphrey, Thomas Spencer and Hills Taylor, the father of B. F. Taylor. Mr. Taylor drove the four-horse team which hauled the sawed marble to Whitehall, N. Y., the nearest reliable market. He afterward became a marble worker, continuing at it until nearly the close of his life. Following Mr. Taylor, Thomas Derby and Smith Mead were employed as drivers on the Whitehall trips. Mr. Manley was succeeded by C. H. Osborn as foreman of the quarry.

A few rods west of the original Sutherland Falls Mill was the blacksmith shop, later turned into a coping shop, where Hills Taylor worked, and where his son B. F. Taylor learned the rudiments of marble working. This dates back to 1865. Near this shop was the ox barn where a substantial part of the motive power of the industry was housed. In the early years of the mill the only way to get marble up to the track level was to put it on stone boats and trust to the oxen and their drivers. As late as 1880 there were no more than eight or ten horses about the plant and they were driven singly. Nearly all the hauling was done by oxen. The change to horses followed the introduction of a special harness—one in which a single chain displaced the old whiffletrees, thus eliminating the danger of chipping the marble.

The original mill secured its power from an over-shot wheel, which was placed about forty feet below the present level of the railway track. The gangs were suspended by hemp ropes and let down by a crank. In the day of the Dorr & Myers eight-gang mill beside the railway track there was a building between the upper and lower mill levels which was used at different periods as a shop, office and store. It also served temporarily as a dwelling for a man by the name of Daly. When Francis A. Fisher was running the marble business for the North River Mining Co., and living in the Senator Proctor house, he had a room in this building set apart as his official headquarters. It was afterward turned into an office for Hughes & Roberts another of the transitory companies which strove to raise a fortune out of the earth.

Power was first applied to the upper mill by an upright shaft which stood directly back of the Patterson Mill of today. This was subsequently replaced by the inclined shaft which was retained in service until electric power was installed. In the sixties the water at the Falls was turning three different water wheels. It ran into the old mill through a raceway. Leaving there it was coveyed by penstock to another wheel which was set part way down the incline. Then it was sent out again by penstock or raceway to the wheel at the base of the inclined shaft.

The track from the upper mill to the quarries was one of the improvements of 1869. It was later extended to the lower mill by Senator Proctor. At that stage of the industry's development very little filling had been done in the marble yards. The Beaver Pond Brook ran through a gorge south of Patterson's Mill. When the railroad was laid out a culvert was provided

SUTHERLAND FALLS BLOCK PILE, 1885

so that the water might have an outlet, but some of it settled back into the hollow forming a marshy pond. This section of the village straightway took upon itself the rather questionable title of "Skunk Hollow." In certain parts of the yard trestles were required in order to maintain the grade of the quarry track. F. R. Patch, President of the Patch Manufacturing Co., Rutland, and a son of J. L. Patch, recalls that he was working with his father on one of these trestles while Chicago was burning.

Blocks were let down over this track by a cable and the working of this cable and the machinery connected with it was the source of endless creaking and rumbling. When Mr. Patch was a boy living in his father's house at the foot of Patch Hill, the youngsters of the neighborhood gave another interpretation to the rolling of the cable. To them it was the thunder of the mountains.

Supplementing the work of his father, F. R. Patch was an able participant in the construction work which went hand in hand with the growing business. He built the present Senator Proctor house. (The first house on that lot was burned in 1883.) He reared a home for himself on South Street, the place which is now being utilized as a Catholic Rectory. The mills north of the first stone mill on the upper level were raised under his supervision. When the mills were finished he was employed for a time as mill foreman and later he was made general superintendent. He was the designer of the Proctor Union Church.

In the sixties the Sutherland Falls Quarry was barely twenty feet deep and the men went in and out on ladders. The sand bank known as "Benson Hill" extended nearly to the railway track. A store stood

CARPENTER SHOP, 1922, FORMERLY THE SITE OF SUTHERLAND FALLS BLOCK PILE.

between the railroad and the sand bank and there was hardly room to get around it. This store was the nucleus of the Proctor Cooperative Store, the birth and upgrowth of which will be treated in another chapter.

The first marble finishing undertaken by the Company in 1876 was the turning of urns. The shop stood on ground now covered by the monumental boxing room. A man named Gilbert was shop foreman.

Work of this kind had been inaugurated at an earlier period by the Columbian Marble Company and to that concern goes the credit for operating the first lathes in Vermont.

Altogether there have been three monumental finishing shops in Proctor.

In December, 1885, on one of the coldest nights of the season, the shop, boxing room and station were counted out by fire. The cry was raised at eleven o'clock with the thermometer fixed at 15 degrees below zero. Little could be done under such conditions except work for the safety of the adjoining buildings and make plans for a continuance of the work of the shop. As a temporary makeshift a lease was secured of the Baker Mill at the Double Roads Crossing. This was the center of the combined finishing activities while machinery was being bolted into place in the building shop and in the north end of Haley's Mill.

The second monumental shop extended northward from the site of the burned structure to the one-story mill. It was also reinforced on the south by a twenty-four gang mill, which, except that it had only one story, is duplicated by the Johnson Mill of today.

Two or three pages in the scrap book are dedicated to the second Proctor fire. This quotation from the Rutland Herald, dated July 3, 1894, tells something of the struggle of that hazardous night:

"Fire started about midnight in the main mill of the Vermont Marble Company at Proctor. The fire spread with great rapidity, and at one time it seemed as though the entire mill was doomed. The building is 400 feet long, 80 feet wide and two stories high. The finishing shop and the new mill were entirely destroyed. The contents included 24 gangs of saws and a large amount of marble in process of preparation for the market. At 1:30 o'clock the fire threatened to spread from the finishing shop to the Patterson and Haley mills. The mills were all under one roof and strenuous efforts were made to check the fire at that point. Scores of men were on the roof with buckets of water, while other men erected barricades of marble against the tin covered partition doors which connected the different mills. President Fletcher Proctor personally superintended the battle at this point. At two o'clock the steamer from Rutland arrived and was greeted with a cheer from the large crowd. Hose had been laid from a point on the creek directly back of Senator Proctor's house to the critical point of the fire. By this means, and through the efforts of the bucket brigade, the fire was kept from spreading beyond the heavy partition walls at the north end of the finishing shop."

In this second interval of rebuilding the business of finishing was carried on in the shop at Center Rutland and in the old Sheldon Finishing Shop at West Rutland. Prior to the loss the Company had 16 mill gangs idle in Proctor and 75 in West Rutland, so that the question of sawing was of negligible import.

These two conflagrations are not the only ones which the Company has had to withstand, but they are the ones which left the deepest scars. In January, 1907, the cooperative store at Center Rutland was cut off by the fire king. In later years the mills at Beldens and Brandon have gone the same way. In August, 1915, a fire at West Rutland blotted out the carpenter's shop and several storage buildings. Yet in none of these instances has the entire plant been threatened as in the case of the monumental shop fires.

Within the memory of Mr. Taylor the flat roofed mill on the lower level wore on its forward crest a row of diminished marble spires which flaunted themselves in the air like the feathers of an Indian's head-gear. The purpose of this display was to tell the passengers on the leisurely moving trains of the work that was going on there in the valley and to suggest some of the uses to which marble was being applied. It is obvious, therefore, that the marble workers of that day were not unmindful of the power of advertising.

Nor must it be assumed that no previous attempt had been made to create publicity for Vermont marble. The Rutland Herald of 1848 carried an advertisement of Davis, Morgan & Company, which featured in highly colored bombastic phrases the marble from the celebrated West Rutland quarries. Perhaps the campaign was started even before that time.

One fact seems to have been positively established: the work of the monumental salesman in those days was most indefinite and unfruitful. Henry Donnelly, a resident of Proctor since 1875, and the first occupant of the Serri house, has kept in mind some of the reminiscences of T. J. Ormsbee. Mr. Ormsbee was one of the first salesmen in the Rutland section, and he maintained that it was not enough simply to do the selling. One never knew whether a sale meant money or merely an exchange of commodities. Things as diversified in value

VERMONT MARBLE COMPANY, 1890

and utility as an old Continental Army uniform and a bear trap were handed over to him in payment for tombstones.

In the spring of 1876 the Company built a two-story stone mill of 12 gangs. This was the north section of the Patterson Mill, where the stairs lead up to the sand tramway. It was set on a ledge and men were at work there during the winter of 1875-76, blasting and cutting to get a foundation. In 1880 work was commenced on the first section of Haley's Mill. The other addition to the northward was made about two years later. Under the north end of Haley's Mill was a gulch fully 100 feet deep.

It was related by John D. Andrews, who arrived in Proctor in 1875, that when he began work here one twelve-foot rubbing bed was all that was owned or needed by the Sutherland Falls Marble Co.

The first Building Shop went up in the summer of 1880, the site being very nearly identical with the present shop. It was 100 feet long and 56 feet wide. Additions and changes were made from time to time so that the Building Shop of 1922 is quite a different structure. The first foreman of exterior building was Thomas Hagan, father of Dr. Hagan of Pittsford. The first cutters, fifteen or twenty in number, were brought here from Boston. The first large building exterior to be cut in Proctor—the State Capitol at Indianapolis, Ind.—was produced in 1881. It included 72 polished marble columns thirteen feet high and two feet four inches in diameter. The second building shop foreman was James Edson, since deceased, a brother of Albert W. Edson. After that, A. C. Freeborn was made superintendent of exterior building with J. D. Andrews as the third foreman.

The first Italian cutters to work in Proctor were Dante Bacolli and A. Fabiani. Two more came a little later, Tony Parini and Frank Balduci. These men have all left town, although Mr. Fabiani has a daughter here, the wife of A. Zambelli.

The first Swedish employe in Proctor was Lars John Larson. Senator Proctor hired him in New York, a Swedish imigrant just in from the old country. Larson worked here for about eight years, beginning in 1870. He finally left the Company to become a Maine farmer.

In 1875 the Company's Machine Shop was near the Sutherland Falls Quarry. It was equipped with only a few machines. Later a shop was opened on the second floor of the Steel Building. The Carpenter's Shop was in its present position. The Company's Barn was in the hollow north of the Old Library Building. Teasdale was then foreman of the finishing shop and Matthews was mill foreman, and it is with the initials of those names "T" and "M" that stock for those departments is still being marked.

The road of that day skirted the ledge west of the Senator Proctor place, continuing north on the east side of the railway track, turning at right angles west of Stillson's rubbing beds, and bearing northwest toward the present machine shop. North of the machine shop was a stone bridge for the crossing of Beaver Pond Brook, and from that point the road passed back of the carpenter shop where it joined the market road at the corner by the Swedish Boarding House.

It was in 1885 that the Company's Office of today began to take form. The building then being used for that purpose was north of the store and the store was where the rubbing beds and shipping office now stand, flanked on the one side by the coping shop and on the other by the railroad. In front of the store was the track where the blocks were let down from the quarry. In the upper mill yard was a turn table where the blocks for the lower mill were switched off and sent down under the storage building and finishing shop to the end of the track. South of the string of mills on the office level was a small shed used as a coping shop; next to that was the building for storage and boxing; then the monumental shop; and beyond that the rail-way station—if indeed anything so small can be allotted so large a name.

Under the same roof with the monumental shop were the library and the grist mill—a somewhat un-harmonious combination. The grist mill was in the basement, or in that part of the structure which jutted down to fit the slope of the hill. Over that was the cutting shop. On the upper floor in front was the libra-ry with the polishing shop in the rear. It will be under-stood, no doubt, that the library section, during work-ing hours at least, was for the storage of books rather than for reading.

The dedication of the new office in 1886 marked a span of fifty years in the marble industry at Suther-land Falls, and of the many men who had charge of operations there, only one, Redfield Proctor, had the insight and the tenacity to lift the business out of the invalid class and give it health and prosperity. It would be futile to write of the qualities of leadership with which Mr. Proctor was endowed. All this has been set forth with unmistakable clearness by men who knew him and worked with him. There are however a few little incidents related by some of the older employes of the Company which illumine, each in its own peculiar way, well defined phases of his character.

VERMONT MARBLE COMPANY'S POWER HOUSE REPLACED BY
HYDRO-ELECTRIC PLANT IN 1905

One man avers that while the Senator expected his employes to keep at work, he was always ready to work with them, and in any kind of weather. On rainy days he simply combined a long coat with his wide-brimmed hat, and if anyone remonstrated with him against staying out in the yard he would argue that it was the best time for yard work, as the cracks in the marble were most easily detected in wet weather.

Then there is the story of the balky horse. In the seventies, or possibly the early eighties, the Company had an exceedingly temperamental horse which was used to draw sand to the mills and deliver goods from the store. Sometimes he would go but quite often he would stay. The Senator made a survey of his forces and told a certain driver named Haley to try the horse, intimating that if he failed to make him go the animal would be sold. It so happened that Mr. Haley had been placed in charge of a gang of laborers and had no relish for the new job. The Senator had advised putting on a light load at first, but instead of that Haley shoveled on all the wagon would hold. Moreover, he dug holes under the wheels in order to make the start still more laborious. Then, climbing up to the seat and picking up the lines loosely, he suggested to the beast that it was time to start. He expected that the horse would stand there indefinitely and that he would be permitted to return to his men. But altogether to his surprise and disgust, the animal walked away with the load unhesitatingly, whereupon James Haley was asked to continue as its driver. This he did, indeed, for several years, until he threatened to leave if no other work was available. It was decided on the strength of his experience that the horse had a tender mouth instead of a balky disposition, and that

VERMONT MARBLE COMPANY'S POWER PLANT

Haley, by not trying to drive it, had accomplished what could never have been gained by more vigorous tactics.

In 1871 James Haney and five or six other men appeared before Senator Proctor and asked for a job. He agreed to give them work for two weeks. He told them that times were hard, yet at the same time he emphasized the fact that he had never discharged a good man. Mr. Haney did odd jobs around the yards during those two weeks, and for some time thereafter. Finally, in the early part of December, the Senator came around and told Haney that he had just let a lot of old men go and asked if he thought he could get a job on a farm for the winter.

"I can try," replied Haney.

"I'd like to have you come back in the spring," the Senator assured him.

"I can't promise that," said Haney. "Has my work been satisfactory?"

"Yes," answered the Senator.

"I thought you told me you never let a good man go," Haney reminded him.

The Senator had started to walk away but at that he turned around.

"Well, I haven't, have I," was his unruffled rejoinder. And Mr. Haney has only lately been placed on the Company's pension roll after fifty years of service.

Possibly it was in the handling of men more than in any other one capacity that Senator Proctor displayed his genius for business. Not alone in picking good men, but in keeping them, was he a master of industrial methods. And he was ready at all times to do his part toward raising men to an efficient standard. Mr. Powers has on record the case of a man discharged for drunkenness, whom the Senator agreed to take

back if he would give five dollars to every poor widow
in town. It was estimated that the price of his rein-
statement on that basis would be about thirty-five
dollars. And with an eager "I'll do it," the man accepted the terms and returned to work.

In Mr. Partridge's address is a brief analysis of
the careers of both Senator Proctor and his son, Fletcher
D. Proctor. He explains how one as founder and the
other as the organizer were adapted to the work of their
respective periods—how each gathered unto himself
the men who were needed to systematize and bring
into harmony many scattered departments. All this is
ably summarized in the St. Albans *Messenger* of Feb.
5, 1902, in an editorial which was inspired by the reorganization of the Company corporation.

"From its inception," the writer declared, "the
Vermont Marble Company was a Vermont enterprise,
instituted by a Vermont man, a typical Green Mountain Boy, Redfield Proctor. Those who know the inner
details of his first experience in the marble business
can tell something of a story of home industry, pluck
and perseverance, sometimes in the face of discourage-
ments, but always and ever supported by character-
istic determination, fixity of purpose and lofty aspira-
tions that must eventually break or be broken. There
could be no other reason than that the Company
flourished, no other outcome of the brains, patience,
and industry that fathered it, but that the foundation
should be laid for the largest marble quarrying and
finishing business on the globe. But if Redfield Proctor
laid the foundation, the second generation reared the
structure to its present proportions. To the young men
who became interested in the business from time to
time, the elder Proctor gradually relinquished control

of the management, and for the past few years, he has made no pretense whatever of knowing anything about it. The far-reaching ramifications of this great industry are today the immediate results of young Vermont brains and stick-to-it-iveness, the work of "The Boys" as Senator Proctor proudly calls them. This institution was conceived in a Vermont brain, and literally built out of Vermont rock by Vermont men. It is distinctively of and for Vermont in all its parts and aspects, and the Vermont spirit behind it could not complacently see it masquerade longer behind a New York charter— We need in all our business circles the same enthusiastic loyalty to the 'Vermont Idea' that has ever animated and inspired the personnel of the Vermont Marble Company."

It would be manifestly incomplete to close this chapter without taking a casual inventory of the present. It is hardly enough to bring the industry up to the year 1922 and then drop it unceremoniously, even though present-day figures may be fairly well known.

The Company now produces about 21,000 blocks annually, owns seventy-five or more quarries, from which are obtained fifty different grades and varieties. The yearly output of marble is approximately 1,000,000 cubic feet. The shops and mills cover a floor space of about twenty-seven acres. In Proctor alone they stretch out to a length of 1,500 feet and there are other plants at Center Rutland, West Rutland, Florence, Brandon, Middlebury, Swanton, Roxbury, Danby, Dorset, Manchester, Bluff Point, N. Y., San Saba, Texas and Tokeen, Alaska. There are branches in many of the more important cities. There are nearly fifty traveling salesmen.

The land owned by the Company, woodland and

AEROPLANE VIEW OF PROCTOR, PHOTOGRAPHED IN THE FALL OF 1922

farms, amounts to more that 26,000 acres. The hydro-
electric stations on the banks of the Otter bring to the
Company's machinery a force of nearly 12,000 horse
power. Each year the Company uses more than 6,000,-
000 square feet of lumber. The number of employees
ranges from 3,000 to 4,000.

In place of the one balky horse which hauled in
the sand from the knoll near the mills, the Company
has substituted an aerial tramway which brings it in
from a huge sand hill two-and-a-quarter miles over
the mountain at the rate of 500 pounds every twenty-
eight seconds. The system was installed in 1900. An
earlier tramway to the foot of Patch Hill had been
constructed in 1894 but the supply at that point was
soon moved into the mills. It was then that the larger
deposit was discovered and the tramway extended.

In a brief sketch of this kind, there is room for
nothing save the larger developments of the industry.
This is not the story of marble; it is the story of Proctor.
Therefore it must concern itself only with those phases
of the business which are of interest to the outsider,
and leave the technical records in the vaults of the
Company. Very few people will care to know when
pneumatic tools and carborundum machines were installed in the shops or when the yards were equipped
with locomotive cranes. The interesting feature of it
is that they have become a part of the industry, that
they are saving labor and working for the prosperity
of the town. Nor would it be worth while to describe
each individual quarry hole within the Proctor limits,
notwithstanding the fact that some of them have a
most tragic history, involving the loss of fortunes and
good names.

An entire chapter might be written on the Lime

Plant, built in 1915 at West Rutland, where quarried marble blocks unsuited for the regular market are being turned into lime at the rate of sixty tons a day. Again there is the system of Company Farms, operated under a partnership plan for the common good of the community. There will be another reference to these farms as the story progresses, but just now it is best to keep land and lime and all other minor issues in the shadow. For, when everything has been said, it all leads back again to the subject of marble.

Well may this chapter be longer and more exhaustive than any of the others. With grist mills and saw mills, Sutherland Falls would have had little chance to raise itself above the level of the ordinary country town. With marble, and the publicity accruing therefrom, it has made itself known the country over and to the lands beyond the seas.

Recognition of this kind sometimes goes to the head of towns as well as of people. Not so in the case of the little marble village at the Falls. The arrival of prosperity enabled it to shake off its old clothes and put on richer and more modern adornment. Yet through it all it clung to its native modesty and simplicity. Change followed change, more perhaps than in any other industrial section of the Green Mountain Country, but none of them had any effect on the town's democracy. It remained quiet and unassuming, living its life decently and doing its work in a sane energetic way.

CHAPTER VI

FROM A SETTLEMENT TO A NEW TOWN

BLASTING AND FILLING—LAYING OUT STREETS AND
BUILDING HOMES—WATER SYSTEMS—LEGIS-
LATIVE STRUGGLES OVER SEPARATION
OF TOWN—PROCTOR IN STATE
AND NATION

THE same monotonous digging, which was required to build the marble plants, was none the less in evidence in the building of the town. There were few level spots available. Nearly all the houses had to be raised on the side of some hill. Although in many instances there were no ledges to dislodge, it was seldom that the work of filling could be even partially curtailed.

John D. Andrews, who was living in 1880 in the house which still bears his name, has given us many pertinent reminiscences of that home-building period.

The Andrews, the Glasson and the Spencer houses, were reared in the fall of 1879, when Henry Woodbury was superintendent of the Company. At that time Mr. Woodbury resided in what is now the Fairbanks dwelling, which had been completed during the previous year. The Spencer home which has recently grown into Ormsbee House, was put up for Mr. Teasdale, the first foreman of the Monumental Shop.

In 1880, High Street, which was then nothing but a road, ran south to the James Glasson place and

VILLAGE SQUARE, LOOKING SOUTH, 1885

ended there. It was the only driveway to the hill. The Patterson house was the first to be built along the line of Pine Street. There was no street there at the time and the timbers were taken up to High Street and slid down the bank.

The christening of Pine Street was brought about in this way. In the winter of 1880, Harry Powers came home from Middlebury College for the mid-year vacation. He had been studying surveying and somehow he learned that Colonel Proctor had a set of instruments. Thinking that he might get a little practice on his father's farm during the recess, he presented himself at the office and asked for the loan of this outfit.

"Yes, you can take it," replied Mr. Proctor, "and if you will come around in the morning, I'll give you a job."

Knowing nothing of what he was to do, Mr. Powers reported at the office the following morning. Colonel Proctor led him out across the marble yard and pointed up through the unbroken tangle of brush and trees. "I want to run a street through there," he said, "I'll show you where I'd like to have it go, then you can survey it."

That was Mr. Powers's first practical experience with the chain and compass; it was also the first street to be surveyed in Sutherland Falls.

There was a big hole east of the Snell house and in order to construct a street they had to cart out three or four feet of black muck and fill the hole with sand. Where Dr. Hack's house stands was a swamp hole with a small brook running through it. The brook bed was filled with cobbles and covered, the cellar being laid above ground. The Hack house went up some years later than the others.

VILLAGE SQUARE, LOOKING SOUTH, 1909

When Church Street was constructed, there was a swamp hole north and west of Forresters Hall. This was filled to a depth of three feet with stone and other material. Apparently, it had a bottom of quicksand, as the filling all settled out of sight after a time and a second lot had to be placed on top of the first. There were no stairs on the hill in those days—only paths. A fence ran west from the foot of the hill, starting near or a little south of the Village Hall, passing south of the Charles Ayers house on Church Street and extending to the land of Hills Taylor, near West Street. This fence swerved to the south around the old stone school house of 1866. During all this time, or until 1875, at least, Hospital Hill was nothing but a pasture.

In those days the residents had to rely on springs for their supply of drinking water. One of the sources was near Tree's Pond, a spot now covered by the Vermont Marble Company's yard. Another was a few feet west of the Rutland railway water tank. This latter spring became useless when, in 1883, the Company built its new barn, the one which is still in use. Still another was northwest of the upper reservoir, at the south line of the Chatterton farm, from which elevation a pipe had been laid to several of the houses in the village.

The first water system, which brought the water of the upper reservoir to certain sections of the village, was put in operation in 1896-7. With this came the first sewerage connection. In 1898 the mains were extended over a larger area, the total cost being about $56,000. The drought of 1899 proved among other things that the upper reservoir was inadequate as a water supply and so the lower reservoir was walled up and connected with a pumping station, so that in case

VILLAGE SQUARE, LOOKING SOUTH, 1911

of emergency it could be forced up into the stand-pipe. This pump was placed in the marble enclosure, which now forms the basement walls of the Lyle Morse house on South Street.

In 1903 the growing village was again calling for more water. Various tests were made in Pittsford and Chittenden, leading to the purchase finally of the site for an intake on Coal Kiln Brook in the latter town. This land was the property of C. R. Holden and from him the village also bought additional rights on Furnace Brook, so that if the need arises another intake can be established above the Holden residence. With this in reserve, no one who lives in Proctor need worry over what he is to drink.

It is like turning the leaves of an old scrap book to listen to some of the stories of sixty years ago, as related by Mr. B. F. Taylor. They are set before us like the pictures in a faded album, each with lifelike fidelity.

First comes Peter Kivelin, or Peter the Sailor, the only laborer in the Sutherland Falls quarry who knew how to splice a rope, a graduate of the old days before the mast, and exceedingly jealous of the knowledge thus acquired. Indeed, so fearful was he that some fellow workman would learn of his methods that he did all of the Company's splicing in secret, even going so far as to tie some of the knots in the night. For recreation he turned to the shore that was nearest at hand and fished for suckers on the banks of the Otter.

Next in line stands Michael Benson, the strong man of the village, who gained his niche in the local hall of fame by carrying a barrel of flour from the store to his home, about a quarter of a mile away. The storekeeper had agreed to give him the flour if he would carry it the entire distance without resting. He ac-

VILLAGE SQUARE, LOOKING SOUTH. 1922

cepted the challenge and literally walked off with the prize. This man Benson had been a well digger in younger life and as proof of his efficiency, he often told of how he had sunk a hole in Chicago to so great a depth that they had to "sound the horn for dinner."

John Dervin, one of the mill workers, was re-nowned as a fox hunter. Mr. Taylor well remembers seeing him trail past the house, a huge fur cap on his head, a muzzle-loading double-barrel shot-gun over his shoulder, a pack of hounds behind him, starting off for a day of sport on West Mountain. Nor was it an empty sport with Mr. Dervin. He turned many a dollar out of his fox hides.

The Beaver Pond of that time and the brook which flowed from there to the Otter, was of real interest to the fisherman. It was in that brook that Mr. Taylor did his first fishing with a bent pin for a hook, a tow string for a line and a rod cut from a neighboring clump of bushes. He declines to give any figures or weights on that first catch; instead he hurries along to a later period and tells of an experience of Dorr and Myers, whose connection with the marble industry has been outlined in another chapter. As a result of the dam they had constructed, both the pond and the trout had grown larger. One summer evening, Mr. Dorr was fishing from the west bank and filling his basket with speckled prizes, which varied in weight from a half pound to two pounds and a half. His partner, Mr. Myers, was fishing from the opposite bank and catching nothing. "As may be imagined," observes Mr. Taylor, "the expressions on the faces of the two anglers were somewhat different."

Living in Proctor today are three men who have witnessed the trasformation of the Sutherland Falls

VILLAGE SQUARE, 1885

that Dorr and Myers knew, into a modern, self-contained, self-governed village. Those men are B. F. Taylor, H. P. Powers and M. C. Warner.

In the midst of this growing period, there arose a contest as to whether the community should administer its own affairs in its own way or be subject to outside handicaps and restrictions. The first step was taken in 1884 when Proctor was incorporated as a village. Then in 1886 a bill was introduced in the Legislature, which proposed to set apart the towns of Proctor and West Rutland. The bill was referred to a special legislative committee and after the introduction of much testimony, the case was argued at length by opposing counsel, one of the pleas for Proctor being made by Hon. William P. Dillingham, who is now United States Senator.

This is not the time to dwell on the details of that struggle; all that need be said is that the bill was passed and Proctor and West Rutland took their places among the towns of Vermont.

The report of the committee recommending the passage of the bill is a much better summary of the evidence than anyone could expect to find elsewhere. It deserves to be reprinted in full in this account of the town's birth, but since there are parts of it which were of greater interest then than they are today, only the more salient paragraphs are being considered. Here then are some of the reasons why Proctor was granted the boon of independence:

"The plan of dividing towns and creating new ones is not novel to our legislation. The Constitution of 1778 gave the Legislature the right to grant charters, constitute towns, boroughs, cities and counties. Less than one hundred of the towns of this State retain their

VILLAGE SQUARE, 1922

original boundary lines intact. Six towns have ceased
to exist and their territory has been divided among
other towns. Since 1783, nineteen new towns have been
incorporated out of other towns.

"Proctor will have nearly ten and one-half square
miles—a larger area than Burlington, Montpelier,
Vergennes, Landgrove and several other towns.

"It will have about 1,724 inhabitants—a number
in excess of about one hundred and ninety other towns
in the State.

"It will have a Grand List of about $10,000—an
amount larger than that of about two hundred other
towns in the State.

"That the proposed town is capable of managing
its own affairs is admitted, and the observations of the
committee fully confirm this. The schools, one of
which we visited, are excellent; the roads, the best in
that section; the village hall, school houses, churches,
public library, the general appearance of the village,
and its character for good order, as expressed by wit-
nesses, are such that it may be fairly called a model
village.

"All of the voters of the Village of Proctor, except
three; all of the farmers in that part of District No. 10,
to be annexed, except one; and all of the voters in that
part of Pittsford included in the proposed town have
expressed such a wish.

"Therefore it may be regarded as conclusively
established, that Proctor has all the elements of a
prosperous, well governed and harmonious town, amply
capable of taking care of itself, and better able to secure
for itself prosperity, temperance and general good
government that it would be under the guardianship
of any other municipality.

LOOKING NORTH FROM OLD LIBRARY BUILDING, 1885

"Proctor village, which is partly in Rutland and partly in Pittsford, is situated six miles north of Rutland village, and separated from it by a purely farming community. The two places are naturally, politically, commercially and socially distinct and separate localities.

"We do not think that a section as distant and distinct as Proctor is from Rutland village should be deprived of the advantages of a town system of government and put into a city against its will. The public wants of the entire people of Proctor are identical, and their welfare would undoubtedly be subserved by being together in one town.

"If the whole town of Rutland was incorporated as a city, two-thirds of the people of Proctor would be in the city of Rutland whose center would be six miles away, while the remainder of the people would would be in the town of Pittsford and subject to an entirely different management of local affairs, which are in reality the same.

"It is exceedingly inconvenient for the people of Proctor to be compelled to go six miles to attend to town business, town and freemen's meetings, primaries, etc. * * *

"The running of the town line directly through the village, thus placing different privileges, duties, and burdens upon a common people is unfortunate and causes confusion. * * *

"The people of this section would be relieved of the inconvenience and unwieldiness of the present large town meetings of the whole town.

"Their local interests and government would be in their own hands instead of being centered in a much larger village, where the majority of the voters are not

LOOKING NORTH FROM OLD LIBRARY BUILDING, 1910

familiar with their wants and needs, and which can not act so intelligently with reference thereto as the people immediately interested themselves. * * *

"It would promote public improvement, * * remove unpleasant differences, * * preserve the town system of government to a considerable people unwilling to be taken into a city.

"West Rutland is divided from the proposed town of Proctor and from East Rutland, by a high range of hills, only once broken and that where the road leading from West Rutland to Center Rutland passes through. West Rutland is four miles from East Rutland, is a thrifty and rapidly growing village. It has six churches, several stores, postoffice and a good railroad depot. The growth of the village is north and south from the center and not towards East Rutland.

"North of West Rutland lies a valley running westerly of the high range of hills alluded to. This valley is four miles long to the northerly line of the town of Rutland, and is a fine farming region, and also contains the principal marble deposits and quarries, which largely contribute to the growth and flourishing condition of this village, containing telegraph, a telephone, and the usual small manufactures and shops for convenience of the people.

"The area of the proposed town of West Rutland comprises about one-third of the whole town of Rutland; population 4,000; Grand List, without exemptions, $21,000; including exemptions soon to be taxed, about $23,000; voters 724, larger than Montpelier in population, with two-thirds as large a Grand List, and more than three times its territory. We found there all the elements necessary to make a first-class town, and we think a city charter embracing the whole town of

LOOKING NORTH FROM OLD LIBRARY BUILDING, 1922

Rutland would be a great injustice to this thriving community, so separated by natural situation from the other villages of the town. The town business cannot be transacted, or the general interest of her people be made identical with the whole town of East Rutland, without great inconvenience and expense.

"All that has been said of the incorporation of the town of Proctor will apply in this case.

"After the division Rutland will have ample territory. In population it will stand second, and in the amount of its Grand List first of all the towns and cities in the State.

"We do not believe that division will injure their business interests or the growth of Rutland village. It will not change the law of trade which seeks the best market regardless of town lines.

"The remonstrants have not, either in testimony, suggestions of Counsel, or in 'points,' suggested any specific injury that can occur to Rutland by the division; and as a matter of right and justice, aside from any material question, Proctor and West Rutland should not be kept in subserviency to a larger town with which they have no social affiliation, whose municipal interests are antagonistic, and from which they are separated by natural boundaries."

In 1888 the new town sent its first representative to the legislature in the person of Redfield Proctor, its friend and benefactor. Mr. Proctor was no stranger at the capitol. He had already served as representative from Rutland in 1867-68, as senator from Rutland county in 1874, as Lieutenant-Governor in 1876 and as Governor in 1878. Consequently, his experience as well as his service, made him the logical choice of his townsmen as their introductory spokesman in Montpelier.

From that time on, Mr. Proctor was largely identified with the political life of the State and Nation.
In 1888 he was chairman of the Vermont delegation at
the Republican National Convention in Chicago and
as an outcome of that gathering he was made Secretary
of War in President Harrison's Cabinet. In 1891 came
his appointment as United States Senator, to fill the
vacancy brought about through the resignation of
George F. Edmonds. To this office he was repeatedly
elected up to the time of his death.

The careers of Senator Proctor and of his son
Fletcher D. Proctor, who was governor of the State
from 1906 to 1908, brought to their home town something that could never have come through the mar-
keting of marble. They brought a respect for the integrity and straightforwardness of the community.
They proclaimed to the state and nation that Proctor
was justified in asking for independence, that as an
individual unit the little town was living up to all
that had been promised or predicted.

In reality, it has been more than the fulfillment of
any prophecy. Looking ahead from 1886, no one could
have been sufficiently optimistic to visualize the Proctor
of today. Any tentative estimate must have fallen
below what has actually been accomplished. So it is
hardly enough to say that the little commonwealth
has made good her claims. The process of "making
good" is still going on and the end is not yet in sight.

CHAPTER VII

THE SCHOOLS AND THE LIBRARY

NO one now living seems to have any definite record of the first school at Sutherland Falls. The most that can be said is that the earliest known seat of learning was on low ground between the river and the elevation which is now occupied by the monumental shop. This building, whatever it may have been called, was available for educational and other public uses until 1836.

It is claimed also that Sutherland Falls had its share of the so-called "select" schools which were prevalent in those days—schools which were organized in private houses and which no doubt often belied the dignity of the name. One such distributor of knowledge was started in the old Warner house where Peter Morganson now lives. Another had its beginning in the Sutherland place.

In 1836, when the optimistic marble operators began to cry for more room, William Humphrey essayed the role of fairy godfather to the children of the village and built for them a new house of learning, a structure which has since been honored with the titles of Old Library Building and Municipal Memorial.

165

In those days the town line between Rutland and Pittsford ran a little north of the section now occupied by Haley's Mill. Although nearly all the buildings were on the Rutland side of the line, the settlement had always been treated as a part of the Pittsford school district. But in 1836 it was made into a separate school district of the town of Rutland, and the stone school house was started with the understanding that it was to be financed by the subscription of the residents. The plan however failed to raise the requisite capital and, in the extremity, Mr. Humphrey furnished the two hundred and fifty dollars which were needed to finish the work. The completed structure was therefore deeded to him, and the title remained in the Humphrey family throughout all the years of its school life. For thirty years this was not only a school house but *the* school house, the only place of its kind in the neighborhood.

The first teacher to preside under this new roof was Jonathan C. Southmayd, a man whose ambition was much too broad for the age in which he lived. He was a graduate of Middlebury College and of Andover Theological Seminary. He was engaged at different times as a tutor in Middlebury and as a teacher in Montpelier Academy. To the people of Sutherland Falls there was naught in his coming except the arrival of another teacher. They had no understanding of the dreams he brought with him of something larger and better than had ever been contemplated.

The house in which he lived was close beside the brook on the edge of the marble yards, somewhat east of the Vermont Marble Company's storehouse. From that home he went forth on week days to train the youngsters in the ways of citizenship and on Sundays to preach to young and old in that same diminutive school room. His spare time was given to private tutoring. It is related that at one time he had under his care and instruction no less than six delinquent college students from Middlebury and Burlington who were looking to him for the knowledge they had failed to absorb in the class rooms. That he had the rare faculty of holding and teaching such men was attested long ago by the parents and friends of the students and in later years by the boys he had inspired.

Thus were his days devoted to work which he regarded as a preparation for the more exacting position he was to fill. Within his vision he could see growing up there in the valley, under his direction, a school of higher learning. In the course of time he secured a strip of land on the slope of Patch Hill and there he proposed to rear a large academy. But his plan had few supporters. Alone and unaided, he began digging and blasting on his plot, that the foundation might be ready when the funds were available. Through the help of E. L. Ormsbee, a brother of Mrs. Southmayd, he collected a pile of marble waste out of which the cellar walls were to rise. Then after two years of service there at the Falls his health began to slip away, and when it was revealed to him that he must leave the cherished labor of his life, he pointed out the spot there on the hillside which was to be his final resting place.

For nearly a hundred years his grave has remained unmolested. It is now closed in by four marble posts and at its head stands a lonely marker bearing the initials "J. C. S." Many houses have sprung up below it. In the near foreground is the residence of C. Ratti. But in the distance is the same glorious Otter Creek Valley, the same color harmony of the mountains

GRAVE OF JONATHAN C. SOUTHMAYD, FIRST PUBLIC SCHOOL TEACHER
IN SUTHERLAND FALLS

VILLAGE SQUARE IN 1912

which Southmayd knew and loved. Altogether it seems quite appropriate that Jonathan Southmayd should sleep where the mountains can watch over him, for there is little doubt that they were an elemental part of his life.

Generous space has been awarded to the sketch of Southmayd's activities not because he was the first or the most efficient of the teachers, but merely because his story is so typical of the early history of the community. He was only one of the many men of that period who were attempting to do something for which the world was not ready.

Of the teachers who came after Jonathan Southmayd, possibly the most famous was Aldace F. Walker, another graduate of Middlebury College, who at the time of his death was president of the Atchison, Topeka & Santa Fe railway system.

Many other names belong on the honor roll of that old stone school house. Emily and Julia Humphrey (aunts of Albert Humphrey), Ellen Warner (sister of Myron Warner), Lucian Palmer, Newall Jenney, Mrs. Hills Taylor and Lucy Powers Cole, the wife of Alander Cole, all had a part in developing the raw material of the pioneer town.

Mrs. Cole was one of the last of these instructors; she was the teacher there in the spring of 1865. So the old building closed its doors to the children at about the time the nation closed its war. Among her scholars at that time were F. R. Patch, H. P. Powers, B. F. Taylor and Christy Moran. They were lined up around the room in long rough board seats, which were made double so that all of the sixty-eight boys and girls could be packed into the room.

It was the overcrowded condition of the school

which started the agitation for more floor space. This led, in 1866, to the erection of another stone school house, a two-story structure, the site of which is now covered by the cooperative store. With the completion of this larger project the village gave up the Humphrey school although the sons of the builder had already offered to turn it over to the district on payment of the original investment of $250. Thereupon it was sold to Fayette Vaughan, one of the marble men of that period, who turned it into a tenement. It was occupied during the twenty-five years following 1868 by some of the superintendents and employees of the marble works. It was the home for a time of F. R. Patch, bringing to him the singular experience of living as a man in the rooms where he went to school as a boy. It remained in the residence class until 1888 when it was converted into a public library.

It took about two years to get the second school in operation. Masons from Rutland laid the stones and J. L. Patch & Son had charge of the woodwork. The keystone over the front entrance, which bore the inscription "A. D. 1866", was cut by B. F. Taylor. The walls literally rose out of a swamp, the natural level of the old village center being very much lower than it is today. The marshy character of the ground led some of the voters to complain that it was unfit as a site but notwithstanding their opposition the work was pushed through to a triumphal finish. The stone addition of 1866 was in use until 1903, and not until 1914 did it cease to be a part of the village.

While these two schools each in its own time ruled alone within the village, there was another district at the Double-Roads Crossing supported by the homes of that neighborhood. Here again, dates are hard to pro duce but it must have been early in the nineteenth century when the first building, which is remembered as a structure of either six or eight sides, raised its head in the valley.

It stood on the south side of the road west of the present bridge. It was reduced to kindling wood in 1872.

Then arose a controversy as to where the new one should stand. The men of the district were unable to agree on a site. For a year or more there was no school at the Double Roads. Then the women took a hand in the fight and called in the selectmen of Rutland. They all met together in the covered bridge and one of the selectmen made a short but impressive speech which was worded somewhat as follows:

"You have got to have a schoolhouse and it can't be built up in the air. You will have to locate it somewhere on the ground."

This philosophy apparently was not without its effect, for in 1875 a new school was established on the north side of the road nearly opposite the old foundation. Thus was opened another chapter of school history in District No. 10. At the end of thirty-five years the second building was discarded and the scholars were transfered to the village of Proctor.

By that time Proctor had entirely outgrown the old stone school-house of 1866. It had added unto itself the North School which went up in the summer of 1883, the Village Hall school, a product of 1886, and the South School, which was reared in 1903, the very year in which the stone school house closed its doors and passed into an inactive old age. This expansion of the educational life of the village was but a reflection of the prosperity of the marble business and the stable growth of the community.

TOWN HALL OR VILLAGE SCHOOL, BUILT IN 1886

TOWN HALL, WITH ADDITIONS BUILT IN 1897 AND 1909

With the dedication of the Village Hall structure began the life of the Proctor High School. In 1892 it presented diplomas to its first graduating class, and year by year the classes have increased, both in numbers and efficiency, an efficiency born of higher standards and better equipment.

Looking back over the old reports, one gets the impression that ever since the days of 1836 the school directors have been asking for more room. Yet there has always been reason in their asking. They remodeled the central building in 1897, and again in 1909, when the new Village Hall was built. They added the Patch Hill school in 1914. And still there was insufficient space at command.

The last move was made in 1919, when the new High School was conjured up from the rocks and given the place of honor on the hill. All this needs no explanation or description. Everyone knows what is comprised within those stately brick walls and what it all represents. The cost of the undertaking was about $60,000, but why speak of it as though it had a cash equivalent. A better way is to look only at its wonderful capacity for service. Then it can be seen as it really is—a great asset for the present, a priceless heritage for the future.

Not alone in itself is the new High School well appointed for the great task to which it is dedicated. The entire cap of the hill has been transformed into a modern playground, so that it stands in its completeness far above the level of the ordinary country town. The work of grading and equipping the grounds was a private contribution to the Proctor school system, the gift of Miss Emily D. Proctor.

Cavendish House and Ormsbee House are two other comparatively new institutions which have been

HIGH SCHOOL

established and maintained by Miss Emily D. Proctor and Mr. Redfield Proctor. They are being set aside for another page. Each must be regarded as an educational unit of commanding interest, yet, with their manifold activities, they seem to insist on another kind of setting. Consider them as dismissed for the present, therefore, while the story trails back to the first days of one of the school's best allies—the library.

*   *   *   *   *

The old Monumental Shop Library was inaugurated in 1881, with few books on its shelves and little money in reserve. Those few volumes, a number that was all too small for the growing list of readers, were kept on the jump from house to house, and with each visit the appetite for more grew harder to subdue. It was this craving which led in short order to a definite organization for the uplift of the reading idea.

In the first record book of the club is this preface: "We, the subscribers, associate ourselves together under the name of the Proctor Library Association, for the purpose of establishing and maintaining a library within the town of Rutland, in accordance with the provisions of Chapter 1604 of the Revised Laws of Vermont."

This was signed by B. F. Taylor, E. J. Sayre, Fred L. Patch, W. W. Wilkins, J. P. Humphrey, S. W. Mead and John Matthews.

Mr. Taylor was the first president, and, of the original seven members, he is the only one now living in Proctor. Two have died, two have moved to Rutland, one is in Washington, D. C. and one in California.

An annual assessment of one dollar was all that kept the infant book-exchange from being a free library.

Anyone who met that obligation was entitled to take out books. Those few lonely dollars, added to a small number of voluntary contributions, were expected to keep up the shelves and make them interesting.

Through the help of Senator Proctor, however, the library managed to elude the perils of babyhood and grow into a fairly normal youth. It was his custom to double whatever amounts the association might raise for the purchase of books, and on many other occasions it was largely through his efforts that the wolf was driven away from the door of the treasury.

After a few years it was thought best to take the books out of their monumental setting and give them a home that was more quiet and congenial. They were transferred to the upper floor of the Company's store, where the rumble of machinery was rather less obtrusive and where the villagers could find their way in without dodging the marble blocks. There the library gathered unto itself an additional stock of books and prestige and overran entirely the partitions which were supposed to hold it in check.

In 1891 the Company called out the masons, carpenters and painters, and told them to make a library out of the stone schoolhouse of thirty-six. That was the year when the marble approach was set in place and the inside partitions gave way to shelves and alcoves. It was most natural that the books should become attached to those walls wherein Southmayd had taught and the call had come to the patriots of sixty-one. There they remained for more than twenty years. There they would doubtless be today had it not been for the kindly foresight of Mrs. Emily J. Proctor. For the brick edifice across the river is her gift, a helpful offering to the booklovers of all ages.

In May, 1913, when the books made their final pil-
grimage, the old library building was left once more
in a state of inactivity. Nor did there seem to be any
insistent demand for the kind of service in which it
had spent its days. For a time it simply clung to the
corner of the square, an empty shell without plan
or purpose. Then, in the days following the Great
War, it came into its own again in a large and glorious
way. It was bought from the Company by Mr. Redfield Proctor, given complete restoration and an artis-
tically finished interior, and presented to the village as
a Municipal Memorial and a home for the American
Legion.

Speaking at its dedication, May 29, 1920, Mr.
F. C. Partridge made this reference to its historic
significance:

"This building combines in happy measure many
things desirable in a memorial. It is practical and useful. The village and town will henceforth have one of
the most attractive and practical buildings for official
uses of any town in the state. Locally it perpetuates
the memory of the simple beginnings of the town, its
early striving after education, the pioneer days of the
library, and the commencement of the marble industry.
Beyond and above these purely local things, it is intended to preserve the memory of the loyalty and de-
votion of those who from our town went into military
and naval service during the Great War. In the main,
or memorial, room there is to be a tablet with the names
inscribed thereon of those heroes, and in his deed of
gift to the village, Mr. Proctor has provided that the
local chapter of the American Legion may keep its
records in the building and may use the memorial room
for its meetings and gatherings."

THE PUBLIC LIBRARY IN 1895

Returning again to the new library, it would be a waste of space to tell what it is and how it looks. Nine years have slipped away since the day of its opening, and they have given everyone an intimate acquaintance with the spacious, restful rooms. The library has already become a loyal and obliging friend—giving freely of its inspiration to anyone who will take the trouble to enter. And of those who come and go the more thoughtful will never fail to pause in reverent respect before the bronze panel which adorns the entrance—an unobtrusive reminder that the building is erected in memory of Arabella Proctor Holden.

If the library could grow in the old days, under the handicap of ungainly surroundings, it could hardly do less in its present environment. And the records show that it has taken full advantage of its larger opportunity. In 1913 it had on its shelves 8,113 volumes, and the circulation for that year was 13,953. At the end of 1921 the stock of books had increased to 12,387, and the circulation was 31,563. This represents not alone a gain in index cards, but, what is vastly more encouraging, a much wider following of the reading habit.

The library is supported by private endowments and contributions, by appropriation from the town of Proctor, and by the proceeds of entertainments given for its benefit. It is managed by a board of directors, in cooperation with Miss Mary K. Norton, the librarian. Miss Norton began her years of service in the old stone building, and it has been under her supervision that the institution has made its greatest advance. Preceding her in office were Elizabeth A. Creer, Nellie M. Glasson, James T. Glasson, Charles W. Glasson, and W. W. Wilkins, all of whom gave unsparingly of their time to the cause.

MUNICIPAL MEMORIAL, 1922, FORMERLY THE PUBLIC LIBRARY

Although few may know of it, the land on which the library stands was dedicated many years ago to the patrons of literature. The old Ormsbee house, which once sat there under the elms, was a home where books were known and cherished, and where others of kindred tastes were ever welcome.

That undoubtedly is the greater reason why a commemorative boulder was implanted in the library lawn. Although the first words on the tablet are a recognition of John Sutherland as the first settler at the Falls, they are overshadowed by that part of the inscription which tells how Mr. and Mrs. T. J. Ormsbee, who once lived there, were "active in good works."

It is through a kindly twist of fortune, therefore, that the last lines of this chapter have been written by Mr. Hamilton Ormsbee, of the Brooklyn Eagle, a son of the old Ormsbee house. No one can travel back with Mr. Ormsbee to that simple cottage without getting a more respectful conception of the library and its mission.

"The library building," he writes, "occupies the site of the house where I was born and made my home until 1875. It was originally owned by a farmer named Pennock, came into the possession of my father, Thomas J. Ormsbee in 1843, and was his home continuously until after the death of my mother in 1890. (The barn on the Pennock farm, by-the-way, which stood a few rods northeast of the present Fletcher Proctor house, was the scene of the first religious meetings held at Sutherland Falls, sometime before the building of the stone school house.)

"My father was a lawyer, had practiced and been postmaster in Rutland, and had gone West to make a home for his family, when he was summoned back

THE LIBRARY

by his brother, Edgar L. Ormsbee, also a lawyer with a taste for geology who had become interested in the marble vein in the valley. Edgar had secured an interest in the marble quarry and the little first mill at Sutherland Falls, and wanted his brother Thomas to take charge of it. My father took the Pennock house and brought his wife there. Four children were born to them there, of whom the two who lived to maturity were Harriett, the late Mrs. Joseph L. Patch, and myself.

"There is still one living link between the new building and the old. My father early in his occupancy trimmed up and staked an elm sapling near his house which had been trampled down by cattle. That elm he often pointed out to me and it is the one which now stands in front of the library entrance. The incident dates the growth of the tree from about 1840.

"My own memories began about 1860, but they include many scenes which show the peculiar fitness of the site to become a public library. My mother was a great reader. Her knowledge of the English classics, indeed, would put to shame most of us today, and the books she and my father had were lent freely to any of the neighbors who cared to read them. When I was eight or ten years old she began reading aloud the novels of Scott in the long winter evenings, a practice which continued for three or four years. One evening, Mr. Smith Warner, our nearest neighbor to the south, came in with one of his boys in the middle of an exciting scene. We begged mother to read on until she got the characters out of their dilemma. With the permission of her guests she did so and they became as much interested in the story as we were. Thereafter the listeners for our evening readings were enlarged by two or three. All I ever knew of Scott I got in that old house by listening and then re-reading the tales I liked best. Father always swore by 'The Antiquary' but mother's favorite was 'The Heart of Midlothian.' I guess mine was 'Guy Mannering.' I know that mother once heard me crying in a violent nightmare and found me going over in my sleep the scene where Meg Merrilies lights the flax in the smuggler's cave. I have often heard mother reproach herself for reading that passage to an imaginative boy before his bedtime.

"At fourteen I went to Rutland to attend the high school and only came home for Saturdays and Sundays. In my first or second winter I came home with some childish ailment which kept me in bed but didn't make me feel very ill. The first morning of that comfortable condition, mother appeared in my room bearing a big red volume, and announced: 'Now, young man, you are going to know some Shakespeare. I am not going to have a big boy like you going around an ignoramus.'

"She began with 'The Comedy of Errors' and I laughed till I cried over the two Dromios. Then followed the comic scenes from 'The Tempest,' the Falstaff scenes from 'Henry IV,' and much of the raillery of Beatrice and Benedick; all things which a boy could enjoy. For years I chose plays for my own reading from which I had heard scenes read aloud, or later, those which I had seen acted. I have heard famous people read from 'Henry VIII' but I have never heard any one put more tenderness and pathos into Queen Katherine than did my mother, reading by the light of a little lamp in that old dining room.

"My mother, however, was not the only reader in the family. My father liked heroic and romantic

WINTER SCENE FROM FLETCHER D. PROCTOR'S RESIDENCE

poetry, Scott, Byron and Campbell. I remember one night when mother was away and he let me sit up late while he read the whole of 'Gertrude of Wyoming' to me.

"My father's passion for thoroughness in his reading met a hard test later, when my mother lost her sight for a number of years and he became her eyes. I came home one Saturday and found him reading a serial instalment of 'Daniel Deronda' to her. I knew he did not like George Eliot, but mother loved her. He read her all of that novel as it came out in Harper's, and everything else, from the newspaper to the Bible, including the Episcopal Church service on Sunday mornings. His occasional enthusiasm for Bible reading shocked his wife. She had been brought up to read her Bible a chapter each day, but when father read it aloud to her he read till he grew tired. One Sunday night he read aloud the whole Book of Job, with comments of interest or sympathy which would have been appropriate to a novel of Scott.

"An early case of his absorption in secular reading was a sore, if brief, trial to his wife. He came home from a business trip one Saturday and said: 'Mother, I've brought you a new book'. It was 'Uncle Tom's Cabin,' and, as mother used to tell the story, she looked forward to a delightful long evening, once she had put her supper things away and seen her children safely in bed. When that time came, however, she found father deep in the story and in no mood to lay it down. Mother waited for him to grow tired, but finally gave up and went to bed. Father kept right on until the last page of the story was finished, somewhere before daylight in the morning.

"Can any one imagine a more appropriate place for a public library than on the site of a home saturated with the love of reading as was that one? I can believe that gracious founder of the Proctor Library could have no better wish for its usefulness than that the spirit of the home which it has replaced should become incorporated in the new and handsome building, inspiring those who seek to make it helpful and blessing those who take advantage of its opportunities."

CHAPTER VIII

THE STORY OF THE CHURCHES

EARLY SERVICES IN PENNOCK BARN——LEMUEL HAYNES——
THE CHAPEL——THE UNION CHURCH AND PARISH
HOUSE——ST. DOMINIC'S CHURCH——GREEK
CATHOLIC——SWEDISH LUTHERAN——
SWEDISH CONGREGATIONAL

IN Mr. Ormsbee's sketch there is a reference to the religious services which had their beginning in the Pennock barn. One of the worshippers at that early shrine was J. C. Powers, the father of Harry Powers, and it is a tradition of the family that the first of those meetings must have taken place prior to 1830. Nor were they limited to sessions of preaching; the Sunday School also began under that roof. An old circular marks the year as 1821.

The first minister to interest himself in the Sutherland Falls community was the Rev. Lemuel Haynes, a colored preacher, whose life was strangely interwoven with the church history of the Vermont pioneers. Chauncey K. Williams, in his address at the Rutland Centennial Celebration of 1870, has this to say of the man from the South, whose lot it was to spend his days in the northern wilderness:

"Rev. Lemuel Haynes, in his day and generation, was one of the most remarkable men of Vermont. Fifty years hence, it may be, and probably will be, difficult to apprehend the difficult position in which not

187

only he, but also the people of that parish were placed in employing such a clergymen to minister unto them. Mr. Haynes was a partially colored man, his father being of unmingled African extraction, and his mother a white woman of respectable parentage. His name was neither that of his father or mother, but (probably) that of the family under whose roof he received his birth. He was born at West Hartford, Conn., July 18, 1753. When he was five months old he was carried to Granville, Mass., and bound out as a servant until he was 21. During a revival he became a professor of religion, and being persuaded that it was his duty to become a preacher of the Gospel, he commenced the study of the ministry with Rev. Daniel Farrand of Canaan, Conn., and on the 29th of November, 1780, he was licensed to preach. On the 9th of November, 1785, he was ordained to preach at Torrington, Conn., the Rev. Daniel Farrand preaching the sermon. After remaining in Torrington a short time he took a missionary tour through Vermont, at the request of the Connecticut Missionary Society. The result of this trip was that he was invited to settle in West Rutland, where he remained till May, 1818, when he was dismissed. From here, Mr. Haynes went to Manchester, where he remained three years, and in February, 1822, removed to Granville, N. Y., where he passed the last eleven years of his life, dying there on the 28th of September, 1833."

In observance of the twenty-fifth anniversary of the Union Church of Proctor, an event of the year 1915, Rev. F. W. Raymond, who was the pastor at that time, issued in pamphlet form a short historical sketch which reaches back over the first epoch of development. This sets forth with great clarity the various happenings of the years, illuminating the path from the Pennock barn to the marble structure on the other side of the river. It needs only a bit of pruning here and there and a few lines pertaining to later incidents to adjust it to the pages of this book.

It begins with the Pennock meeting place and designates Mr. Haynes as "one of the men sent out shortly after the Revolution by the Connecticut General Association of Congregational Churches as missionaries into 'ye settlements now forming in the wilderness to the westward and northwestward,' namely New York and Vermont.

"Later" it continues, "a small school house, situated near the Sutherland Falls, was used for many years for religious purposes. The Humphrey school house (Old Library Building) was built in 1837 and there, among others, Rev. Jonathan C. Southmayd, a graduate of Middlebury College and Andover Seminary, taught, and on Sundays conducted religious services. Congregational ministers from Rutland, West Rutland and Pittsford also preached there from time to time. After the erection of the old stone school house (1866-8) services were held more regularly, the community having at that time about 300 inhabitants. This building (recently torn down) was located on the site now occupied by the Vermont Marble Co.'s store."

Once, while services were being held in that old school house of 1866, the entire congregation was drawn outside by cries from the hill a few rods to the eastward. The Hewitt boy had fallen out of an apple tree and broken his leg. There was no doctor in the village in those days, so a messenger was sent out posthaste to the adjoining town. By the time the man was back, Senator Proctor had the injured bones in place

THE SCHOOL HOUSE OF 1866, WHICH SERVED ALSO AS A HOUSE OF
WORSHIP

and there was nothing for the doctor to do. All this
may be aside from the subject of churches, never-the-
less, as a preachment on the versatility of the town's
founder, it is a pardonable intrusion.

"Ministers from the denominations represented
in the neighboring towns served the community. Cottage prayer meetings were held from house to house.
As the settlement grew, it was felt there should be a
building erected for church purposes, and in 1880 a
chapel was built by an association formed under the
laws of Vermont, on land now owned by the Union
Church. In early meetings, there was much discussion
over the name of the Association, 'Sutherland Falls
Chapel Association,' 'Sutherland Falls Ecclesiastical
Association' and 'Sutherland Falls Union Association,'
being all finally rejected and giving way to 'The Union

Chapel Society.' In the chapel, ministers of different denominations and from different communities conducted services. Sessions of the Sunday School were held there during the summer months, until April 8, 1883, when the Sutherland Falls Sunday School was organized. From about 1884, the building was used also by the Swedish Lutheran and the Swedish Evangelical (Congregational) societies.

"On March 3, 1889, the chapel was destroyed by fire. Plans for continuing the work were discussed and on June 3, 1889, a meeting was held in the Village Hall to consider (1) rebuilding the chapel, (2) organizing a Union Church. On June 11, 1889, a committee which had been appointed to look into the matter reported. The Union Church Society was formed and a board of stewards elected to see about plans for a church building and funds for its erection. September 11, 1889, plans for a building were submitted and it was voted to begin work. In April, 1890, Rev. L. A. Bigelow, of the Troy M. E. Conference, was secured as pastor. On June 11, 1890, one year after the Society was formed, a meeting was held in the Village Hall to consider forming a church, and a committee was appointed to draft a manual and to consult with such persons as might desire to unite. On June 18, the committee reported, and a clerk, a treasurer and four deacons were elected. On July 6, 1890, the members were formally received into the church at the first communion service—42 by letter, 13 on confession of faith, a total of 55.

"On May 11, 1890, the corner stone of the church building was laid by Rev. L. A. Bigelow and visiting clergymen, the address being given by Rev. C. C. McIntire of Pittsford. On December 31, 1890, the

first service, a Y. P. S. C. E. prayer meeting, was held
in the church. On September 27, 1891, the building
was dedicated. A sermon was preached at the morning
service by Rev. W. W. Foster, Jr., and another at the
afternoon service by Rev. J. W. Bixler, of New London,
Conn. Such were the beginnings of the Union Church.

"In 1899, Mrs. Redfield Proctor gave to the church
the present comfortable and commodious parsonage
and the ground on which it stands.

"The growth of the parish and the growing needs
for social and Sunday School work made a parish house
seem almost a necessity. Funds began to be gathered
for that object; the clearing of the debt and the organization of a Brotherhood gave further impetus. June
9, 1910, work was begun on the present parish house and
on January 24-25, 1911, it was dedicated. It has indeed
met a real need.

"In the 25 years of its history the church has had
but four pastors; Rev. Loyal A. Bigelow and Rev.
Howard J. Banker coming from the Troy M. E. Conference; Rev. George W. C. Hill, from the First Congregational Church, New Bedford, Mass.; and Rev.
Frederick W. Raymond, from the Congregational
Church, Hamilton, N. Y.

"The growth in membership has been steady and
continuous. To the original membership of 55, there
have been added 147 on confession of their faith and
182 by letter, making a grand total of 384. There have
been removed from the membership by death, 33; by
letter, 134; and by dismission and revision of the roll,
8; a total of 175; leaving a present membership of 209.
The resident membership is 156. Those who have come
into membership have come out of many different
denominational trainings, such as Baptist, Episco-

THE UNION CHAPEL, BUILT IN 1880, BURNED IN 1889, AND REPLACED IN 1891 BY THE PRESENT UNION CHURCH

palian, Roman Catholic, Presbyterian, Reformed Presbyterian, Dutch Reformed, Reformed Church of Hungary, Congregational, Disciple, Universalist, Methodist, Evangelical and others. They have come, too, out of many lands. There have been baptized in the parish some 207 adults and children.

"This statement of 'Principles' is taken from the Manual:

"This church shall be Congregational in its form of government and discipline in accordance with the legal interest of the society with which it is connected.

It will seek the relations of Christian fellowship with other evangelical churches, by the mutual transfer of members, by ministerial exchanges, by sacramental communion, by mutual councils, and by all suitable modes of cooperation, and in its action in pursuance of these principles, it does not intend to merge itself in any denominational organization.

"Before there was a Church there was a Sunday School. Its sessions were held in the summer months until April 8, 1883, when the Sutherland Falls Sunday School was organized. After the building of the church, the Sunday School became identified with it. The importance of the Sunday School has always been recognized and effort has been made to keep it abreast of the times in methods and efficiency. With some slight falling off in the middle period, there has been an almost steady growth in membership and attendance. Last year the average was 185. The past few years the school has taken a vacation for one or two summer months, it is believed with wholesome effect on both attendance and interest during the rest of the year. The school is now graded somewhat along the line of the public schools, and the International Graded Lessons are in use in most of the classes. It is divided into three separate departments, meeting on Sunday noon; the adult department meeting in the church, the intermediate department on the main floor of the parish house, and the primary department down stairs in the parish house. Effort is made to provide a competent teacher for each class, with an assistant who teaches in the absence of the regular teacher. The Cradle Roll, begun in 1908, has been an important factor in the growth of the school. There is also a Home Department, with a good enrollment, and a class for teachers meeting on a week-night. The Sunday School is a forward looking organization, the hope of the Church, and it is felt that especially in its success in reaching the children of the foreign-born it is doing a real service, not only for the church but for the community and for America. The work of the school is planned and directed by a board consisting of superintendent, assistant superintendent, pastor and two persons elected by the Church.

"On October 18, 1895, the Woman's Home Missionary Society was organized at the home of Mrs. Banker, with this object: 'to aid in interesting Christian women in the elevation and evangelization of needy and destitute women and children in our own land, and in raising funds for this work.' During the earlier years the meetings seem to have been devoted chiefly to missionary programs and reports and to sewing for needy families in Proctor. A 'Dorcas Room' was early established, where garments and supplies were kept. Various causes in this country enlisted the interest of the society and contributions of money and clothing were made. The Kurn Hattin homes early became an object of interest, and the interest has continued through the years. Dr. Grenfell's work on the Labrador Coast has likewise received generous contributions of money and clothing.

"With the growth of the parish, the interests of the society began to extend in other directions. By 1900, the annual chicken pie supper and sale had become an 'institution.' Other suppers, socials and sales have been held from time to time. The annual gentlemen's night has become a delightful feature of the society's year. The first fund of $500 for the erection of a parish house was set aside by the society, when as yet the house

UNION CHURCH

PARISH HOUSE

was but a dream, and was an act of faith. To that, other large sums have been added from time to time, so that the society has a large investment in the parish house and its equipment. This house has made possible a larger work in the meetings. The installation of a 'battery' of sewing machines and complete equipment of the kitchen have made it possible to provide work for a larger gathering of the women of the parish and to conclude each meeting with a very pleasant social hour. In the twenty years of its existence, large sums of money have been raised, with effort and sacrifice, for local benevolences, missionary purposes, the social good of the parish, equipment and repairs in church, parsonage and parish house, and the building of the parish house.

"Other organizations have flourished during the church's history, have made their contribution to its life and have ceased to be. In the early days the Y. P. S. C. E. was a very important factor in its growth. It was organized before the church, September 28, 1889, with seven members, and rendered valuable aid in the organization of the church. The early records tell of the exercise of fellowship through the sending of delegates to local and international conventions, of sending a committee to Pittsford to organize a society, of entertaining children from the city during one or more summers, of raising money for evangelistic work in Rutland County, and of the active interest of those who have ever since carried the church and its work upon their hearts. In 1906, it was felt that the society had served its day and it was disbanded.

"In March, 1893, a Junior Society of Christian Endeavor was organized. It continued until 1899. In 1896, the Junior Society organized itself into a Band of Mercy and gave a portion of its meetings to the consideration of the work of that society. August 29, 1897, it is recorded: 'Our Society has had a partial rest for the months of July and August. The members seemed tired and indisposed to work at the close of last term, so Mrs. Banker said we would have a vacation from committee work until September.' Was this a prophecy of the times that should come in all forms of church work?

"January 25, 1907, a Girls' Missionary Society was organized for the purpose of giving the younger girls some training in missionary interests and in sewing for others. Much excellent work was done during the years of the Society's existence. In 1910, the name was changed to the 'Girls' Aid Society' and in the following year its work was discontinued.

"May 20, 1908, a Brotherhood was organized. Monthly meetings were held for social purposes and many excellent addresses were given by visitors. During the continuance of the Brotherhood and through its efforts, the church debt was cleared, plans were made for a parish house, funds were started and the present parish house was erected.

"Worthy of note, perhaps, are the Church Calendar, which has been published monthly since May, 1908, and the annual Year Book, issued first in 1909, in which are gathered for permanent record the various reports of the year's activities and finances and the revised list of members. In 1904, the church began the happy custom of presenting Bibles to all the children of the parish who had reached the age of seven during the year, and several dozens of Bibles have thus been distributed, many of them finding their way into the homes of the foreign-born.

"Worthy of note, too, would be the many valuable gifts which the Church has received from generous friends. An attempt to enumerate them here would involve the danger of omission. Appreciation is shown in their constant use and enjoyment.

"From the earliest days, the Church began to realize its responsibility for various needs in the community and beyond. The lack of denominational affiliation doubtless had its effect in retarding a growth of missionary interest and effort. For some years, special collections were taken for various objects, mostly undenominational. In May, 1899, it was voted to use the missionary organizations of the Congregational, Methodist and Baptist churches as channels through which to distribute missionary funds. Then for some years the general benevolent fund, gathered through pledges, was divided between these three bodies, Congregational Foreign and Methodist Home (in alternate years, Methodist Foreign and Congregational Home) and Baptist State work. At present, however, the fund is divided annually between the A. B. C. F. M., and M. E. Board Home Missions and the Vermont Baptist State Convention. Effort is made to have each of these causes presented once a year and a special offering is taken for each object. In addition, various other causes are helped from time to time through special offerings and through contributions from the Sunday School and the Woman's Home Missionary Society. There has been a healthy and steady increase in the annual amount of contributions for benevolences.

"A recent Year Book closed with words which are true not only of a single year in the life of the Church but of all its history. Indeed the history of a church cannot be written. It is the life-stories of the men and women

ST. DOMINIC'S CHURCH

GREEK CATHOLIC CHURCH

who have toiled in it, sacrificed for it, and prayed for its welfare. In these, the Union Church has been rich indeed, far beyond the power of words to express or of pen to record. Behind the following paragraph, then, let us have the vision not of a single year but of a quarter of a century:

" 'There are many other things which the Church and the Christians of this parish do which are not written in this book. Some of their ministries can never be recorded in any book. Some of them appear from week to week in the varied services of Christian uplift and helpfulness rendered by such institutions of social service as the Young Men's Christian Association, Cavendish House, the Proctor Free Library and the Proctor Hospital, all of which are helping in manifold ways to make a larger and more worthy life possible—and none of which would ever have been or could be sustained for a single week without that vision of service and that personal consecration to service, born with Christianity and kept alive largely by the continuous ministry of the Church.' "

Since writing these lines Mr. Raymond has become the pastor of a church at Glastonbury, Conn. He has had two successors, the Rev. Caleb H. Hodges, who was called here in 1917 and the Rev. George B. Roberts, who has been minister of the parish since 1919.

These are the notable changes of the later years. The others are not unlike those which may come to any church. One exception, perhaps, is the element of growth, for the advance in all departments has been most energetic and inspiring. The present membership of the church is 269. The Sunday School has an average attendance of 220.

In one respect the Union Church of Proctor is

SWEDISH LUTHERAN CHURCH

SWEDISH CONGREGATIONAL CHURCH

not unlike the store—it is a cooperative institution, where men of many creeds work for one common end. It was an experiment at first, but it long ago cleared itself from the haze of uncertainty. It stands today as a monument to the passing prejudices of sectarianism. Its spirit of brotherliness has been lauded in many parts of the country.

Here again may be detected the pervasive influence of Senator Proctor, both in his own life and the lives of his descendants. Without that, there would, no doubt, have been less of unity and good fellowship.

This thought has been set in enduring form by the designer of the two colored memorial windows which adorn the south wall of the church. In these pictures of glass lies a message for future worshippers which can never be shorn of its effectiveness.

Notice how grippingly the words plead for tolerance and fair-mindedness.

"In memory of Redfield Proctor, the founder of this village and its industry, 1831-1908.
"The strength of the hills is His also."

"In memory of Fletcher Dutton Proctor, 1860-1911. He wrought Christian brotherhood into the community.
"All Israel and Judah loved David for he
went out and came in before them."

This chronicle of the Union Church of Proctor, while it is entitled to the precedence accredited to old age, is only a partial analysis of the religious life of the town. Two Catholic churches and two Swedish churches are assisting, each in its chosen way, to keep alive the tenets of right thinking and right living. It is with full measure of recognition then that the remainder of this chapter is apportioned to them.

"The beginnings of Catholicism in Proctor go back

over three-quarters of a century. In 1848, Reverend Father Daley, the Apostle of Southern Vermont, said Mass in the house of John McLaughlin, one of the earliest residents of Proctor. When a Catholic Church was built in West Rutland, the Catholics of Proctor walked over the mountain to attend Mass and receive the sacraments there. In 1872, the number of Catholics considerably increasing, Reverend Father O'Reilly, of West Rutland, began to say Mass occasionally in Proctor. In the year 1879, Proctor was transferred to the jurisdiction of Reverend Father McLaughlin of Brandon. The question of building a church was raised, and Senator Proctor, who was then governor of the state, promised and gave land, by deed of July 28, 1879, for the church, marble for the foundation, and one hundred dollars in money. The Catholics, though in very moderate circumstances, made a generous subscription. The church was begun in June and the cornerstone was laid and blessed on the feast of St. Dominic, 1879.

"Up to the time of the construction of the church, Mass was said either in private dwellings or in the old stone schoolhouse. The first service to be held in the new church was held on the last Sunday of the year 1880. In May of 1882, on Decoration Day, Bishop DeGoesbriand dedicated the new church.

"Reverend Father McLaughlin attended Proctor from Brandon until 1888. In that year Pittsford and Proctor were formed into a parish, and Reverend P. J. Barrett was appointed pastor, with residence in Proctor. His successors in Proctor were Rev. P. J. O'Carroll, who was in charge about nine months, and Reverend T. R. Carty for two years.

"In 1893 Proctor and Pittsford were separated and

Reverend P. J. Long was appointed pastor of Proctor. During his long pastorate of twenty-three years the Catholics of Proctor were finally organized into a compact and systematic parish. The Reverend W. P. Crosby came as pastor in 1915, and the present incumbent is the Reverend W. H. Cassidy, who was appointed in August, 1921.

"There are in St. Dominic's Parish about twelve hundred souls. Native Americans, of Irish and French extraction, predominate, but there is also in the congregation a considerable group of Italians, Hungarians and Poles. In a very short time, it is expected that a new church, one worthy of the marble center of Vermont, and of the pioneers who have labored so hard in the quarries of Proctor, will be erected."

The Greek Catholic Church of Proctor was erected in the year 1906. At the time of its erection the congregation consisted mostly of Austro-Hungarians. It was organized under the name of "Greek Catholic Congregational Society," and later it was changed into "Greek Catholic Orthodox Society."

The land on which the church stands was donated by the Vermont Marble Company. The Company has also aided the organization in many other ways. During its brief history the Society has been often beset by discord, a blight which none of its ministers has been able to eradicate. It is without a leader at the present time and no attempt is being made to hold services.

The Swedish Evangelical Lutheran St. Paul Society dates back to 1889. In August of that year, the Board of Missionaries of the New York Conference sent the Rev. Mr. Holmes to Proctor to look over the community. At that time was formed the so-called

St. Paul's Society and a student named Karl Martin began holding services in what was then the old town hall. This continued until February, 1890, when the present church was organized under the Constitution and By-Laws of the Augustana Synod. There were 114 charter members.

In November, 1890, the first building was dedicated, all the work of construction having been done by the members.

Since that time, the church has grown constantly in its various organizations, including a large Sunday School. On February 11, 1912, the old building burned, and work was immediately started on plans for a new one. The present structure was completed in 1914.

The Swedish Evangelical Mission Congregational Church was organized September 25, 1888. The real beginning, however, was in 1881, when, largely through the initiative of Otto Ulrickson, the first congregation assembled. In the years between 1881 and 1889, the meeting place was wherever there happened to be available room—in the school house, the town hall, the Union Church and even in private homes. The housing problem was finally solved in 1889, the year in which the present church was built. In the rearing of their church home the members raised what money they could by subscription and borrowed what was lacking. The debt is now entirely cleared. At the time of organizing the membership was 16; at present it is 50.

CHAPTER IX

THE COOPERATIVE STORE, THE SUTHER-
LAND CLUB AND THE HOSPITAL

IT seems like a long journey to go back to the days when store delivery wagons first appeared in Sutherland Falls. Indeed it is difficult to dig out any authorized date and say: "In that year they came." The one outstanding fact is that the early settlers at the Falls had to depend on Rutland or Pittsford for their merchandise and that each purchaser furnished his own delivery wagon.

As the houses began to take their places on some of the vacant lots, it was inevitable that the jealousy of the outside storekeepers should be aroused. The trade of the Falls section was no longer regarded as an insignificant item, but as something worthy of active solicitation. Pittsford, apparently, had the more aggressive spirit for it was from the stores of that town that the teams started to come twice a week to Sutherland Falls, taking orders on one trip and delivering the goods on the next.

This schedule was interrupted finally by the opening of a store at the marble yards. Its site is now marked by the rubbing beds north of the office. It was operated independently by two partners, Messrs. Haywood and Hall. Nothing is available as to the year it was built or the range of its profits and losses. It passed out by the fire route in August, 1872.

While the ruins were still smoking, Senator Proctor planned another store, starting with the old walls as a foundation. In the interim of construction he placed a small stock of goods in a corner of the Company's office, which was then northeast of the coping shop. This temporary store was in charge of Fred Warner, a brother of Myron Warner.

As the year progressed and the building acquired definite form, Senator Proctor began to look about for someone to step in behind the new counters and manage the establishment. If the Company was to have its own mercantile center he must find a storekeeper. The only alternative was to lease the store to some outsider and submit to the risks and uncertainties, which are the natural entanglements of such a course. So confident was he that the right man would be located that he instructed E. M. Sayre, who was then living on the ledge northwest of the store, to make up an order for a car of merchandise with which to relieve the emptiness of the shelves.

In the fall of 1872, Mr. Proctor made an appointment to meet in Rutland a man named Spencer, someone who knew how to buy and sell and who was not then actively engaged. Nothing actually happened at that interview. The matter was left on the table.

"You'll hear from me in about six weeks—one way or the other," said Mr. Proctor.

He did. It was six weeks to a day. And on Dec. 16, 1872, H. E. Spencer arrived in Sutherland Falls and took upon himself the management of the Company Store. The building was virtually finished when he reached town, although the main store room was cluttered with shavings and the various other remnants which mark the carpenter's trail. Men were placed at work immediately, however, to remove the rubbish and bring in the crates and boxes. The shelves were hurriedly decorated with the few products already on hand and by the time the whistle blew that night the doors were open and the store was parceling out provisions to its first customers.

In that way was the Company's Store given its modest start. For two years it was the only place of its kind in the village. At the end of that period, Fred Warner gave up his work with the Company and opened a little store in his own home, a house which was finally converted into the McGary store, an outgrowth of later years.

Mr. Spencer tells us that the lines exploited in that building north of the office were all of the necessity type. Groceries—the staple brands—a little dry goods —still less of crockery—these with a few knickknacks and a few carloads of feed, were sufficient for the needs of the average buyer of 1872.

There was very little cash business. Trade was carried on almost entirely by pass books. At the end of the month, when the men were paid, there were invariably certain ones who would insist on trading out the month's wages in a lump and sometimes for thirty days in advance, if the store was lenient as to the credit.

Nor was there any prearranged schedule for delivering goods. Indeed every patron was his own delivery man, except in the case of flour and other heavy substances. The store had no delivery wagon of its own,

VILLAGE SQUARE, LOOKING NORTH, 1885

but in case of need it drafted either a dump cart or stone boat from the yards.

One day, a woman left an order for a barrel of flour saying that she must have it right away. Mr. Spencer went out to the dock where Senator Proctor had some men loading marble and repeated her instructions.

"We've got to get this car ready," rejoined the Senator. "We can't let the team go now."

"But she says she can't have any supper unless she gets the flour."

"Well, take it along then."

And so the boat was appropriated to drag home the flour and the shipping program was thrown into an intermission.

This incident is more than a mere story. It points graphically to the meagre equipment which was the portion of both the store and the Company when they began the upward climb.

For eight years the original building was considered adequate. Then began the talk of changes and additions. This ended in 1882 when the first section of the store at the southern boundary of the marble yards grew up out of the marshes. It was 100 feet long and 50 feet wide with its longest side parallel to the railway track. Mr. Proctor had been somewhat skeptical about grounding it in a frog pond, but when once the hole was filled and graded and the structure finally in place, it seemed that the problem had been judiciously settled. Room was then available for several well stocked departments, with a reservation of space to meet the inroads of expansion.

No one then contemplated the addition of a furniture department or a tin shop or any of the other varied divisions of trade which were later brought

VILLAGE SQUARE, LOOKING NORTH, 1895

together in the west wing of the store. No one supposed they would ever be needed. But they were.
And so another room 72 feet long and 50 feet wide was
tacked on to the initial building, running to the westward at right angles with the railroad.

Meanwhile, the store building was becoming a
center for other interests. On the second floor was the
library and Odd Fellows Hall; in the basement were
the Garron barber shop and the Post Office, the latter
having been transfered from the Company's Store
in 1882, first to the main floor and afterward to the
rooms below, there to remain until the completion of
the Post Office Block in 1910.

The store has been on a cooperative basis since
1903. Early in the eighties there was a year of ex-
perimenting along this line, a year which aroused all
manner of exaggerated ideas as to the probable size of
the dividend. Consequently at the close of the twelfth-
month there were numerous manifestations of dis-
approval over the result. And so the cooperative plan
was turned back into the files to await a day of kindlier
judgment.

It emerged from its retirement in 1903, although
in a revised and unrecognizable form. Under the new
provisions the Company retained no hold on the profits
of the store. From the earnings of the year were to be
subtracted the operating expenses—rent, merchandise,
salaries—also interest amounting to four per cent of the
capital. Having made these deductions, all that was
left was to be divided among the employees, the share
in each case to be based on the aggregate individual
purchases. As a further stimulus to the undertaking,
the Company named a committee of five employees,
which was to confer with the management on matters
of policy and in the distribution of profits.

VILLAGE SQUARE, LOOKING NORTH, 1922

This was more than a cooperative enterprise, for under any strictly cooperative system the associated members share alike in both profits and losses. In this instance, the Company proposed to say nothing if the store lost money and to hand out whatever it might earn in seasons of prosperity.

As the patrons came to look at the innovation from this angle and observe that prices were as low as in the surrounding towns, they no longer withheld their approval. The Cooperative Store was thus advanced to good standing among the town's institutions.

Spurred on by the expansion of the Proctor business, the Company subsequently opened stores at Center Rutland and West Rutland, both of which through the changes in mercantile conditions, have since been closed, the latter at the beginning of the current year. The Florence Store became another link in the chain in 1911, when that plant was annexed to the Vermont Marble Company.

It would be somewhat premature to allude to the Cooperative Store as we know it today without going back for a moment to that night of November 11th, 1913, when the old wooden structure cast its glare of burning timbers to the far corners of the village. At the time, that fire ranked high as a calamity. True, it brought no little inconvenience, to say nothing of the loss. On the other hand, it was the one thing directly responsible for the new store. Out of it, as from a melting pot, grew a larger and more representative cooperative center for the village.

In one sense, this third and last store is a memorial to the old school house of 1866, for where the one was the other now stands, covering many times over the floor space of the wrecked house of learning. The work

THE COOPERATIVE STORE

AN UNUSUAL VIEW OF THE FIRE OF 1913 WHICH MARKED THE PASSING
OF THE OLD COOPERATIVE STORE

had its inception in June, 1914, and was in progress until March, 1915. Meanwhile, the business of the homeless store was being carried on from several disconnected bases. The grocery department was in the Old Library Building, the drugs and medicines in the Post Office Block, and the dry goods in the Village Hall basement. This was an exacting period for the management. Mr. Spencer was no longer the directing head, and A. G. Dodge, his successor had also withdrawn from the organization. It was left to C. J. Mason, the present manager, to keep the personnel from being disrupted and draw the scattered units together under the new roof.

Anyone who is at all acquainted with Proctor knows more or less about the cooperative store of 1915. The papers of that time alluded to it as "one of the best equipped and most modern buildings of its kind in this part of New England"—a statement which was in no wise exaggerated or misleading. From its exterior of tapestry brick and marble to its underground refrigerating plant, the store is undeniably complete and altogether above criticism.

The phase of its life which is less likely to be appraised is that part which reaches out into the homes of the community. This was most active perhaps during the war period, when saving was the watchword of the day. Many were the ways by which the store sought to popularize the habits of thrift.

The war jostled many stores out of their old-time ruts. To the Proctor establishment it brought only a renewed interest in the welfare of its patrons.

Only the other day a certain prospective customer called at the hardware department to buy a new kitchen range. And this, notwithstanding the fact that he had purchased one within a few years and was needing the money for other things.

"What's the matter with the one you have?" was the inquiry.

"Can't make it work. Got to have another," he insisted.

"All right," they told him, "but you better let us send a man down to look it over. Maybe it can be fixed."

As it proved, the stove had simply been neglected and abused and only a few dollars were required to undo the damage. A sale was lost thereby, but the man was saved the price of a range.

It is in such ways as these that the Proctor store has differentiated itself from others which appear to have similar aims. The average store strives only to exchange goods for cash. Its customers may buy to their last cent without admonition or restraint. But the Vermont Marble Company believes that to be of greatest service the store must be able to view the purchase from both sides of the counter. Then and then only can it do its full duty by the profit-sharer to whom it administers.

* * * * * * * *

The issue of Vermont Association Notes for April, 1913, was a Proctor number, nearly half of the little magazine being given over to an illustrated article on the Y. M. C. A. activities of the marble town. This sketch tells something of the progress of the movement up to that time, and needs only a brief postscript to bring it up to the present.

The opening paragraph is a quotation from one of the newspapers of 1909, the year in which the building was finished and dedicated to its program of service.

"But what of the significance of this new industrial movement?" the writer asks.

"One of the most striking things is the cosmopolitan character of the membership. It is composed of employers, foremen, office men and laborers. It is significant, too, of a growing sympathy between capital and labor. It will help to solve the labor problem, will insure a better quality of work and will develop a higher type of manhood. This building, open to men of all races, classes and creeds, will be a perpetual reminder of the concern of this Company for the moral and physical well-being of its employees."

Then follows the story of achievement:

"In the light of the years just passed this quotation seems like a prophecy which surely has come true. In a town of about 2,750 population it has averaged a membership of about 300. It has been the social center for the young men of the town; it has furnished much of the entertainment of the town; it has conducted yearly evening schools for the non-English speaking men of the town, and been their friend in many ways; it has held successful and uplifting Bible classes and religious meetings for men and boys; it has carried on helpful gymnasium work for men and boys; and it has stood for the best in all things at all times.

"The tenth anniversary was observed on Saturday, Feb. 15. The program was in two sections, the first at the village hall, where a free entertainment of moving pictures and music was given to 600 people. The second part of the programme was held at the Association, with an attendance of 400, and it included a reception, music, games, refreshments, and a splendid exhibit of educational work done this year. The exhibit included architectural and mechanical drawings, clay models,

crayon portraits, posters, landscapes, and other products of the free hand drawing class.

"The Association, built and equipped by the Vermont Marble Company, was opened on February 14,
1903, with an attendance of 800, it being at the time
the first building erected for Association work among
industrial men. It was designed by A. C. Rockwell,
architect for the Company, and cost $36,000, com-
pletely furnished and equipped. Invitations to join the
Association were printed in three languages and 100
men became members in the first hour the building was
open, and 340 joined in the first month, representing
15 nationalities. The first general secretary was J.
E. Baldridge, who came from the Association at Cincinnati, at the opening, and remained about a year,
being succeeded by E. W. Vose, who was secretary for
about three years. He was succeeded by D. R. Mahaffy,
who was a local man, had been one of the directors for
a number of years, and has now been general secretary
for the past six years. E. G. Northrop acted as
assistant secretary, and the physical directors have
been S. E. Abbott, J. E. Elliott, A. B. Cranshaw,
Henry Picord, and Marcus Ling. Fremont Hunter has
been the janitor for ten years.

"William H. Eldridge was the first president, and
served for three years. He was succeeded by George A.
Watts, who also served for three years, and was followed by Benjamin Williams, Jr., the present president.

"Located in the center of the town geographically,
it has always been and now is the center of the male
life of the town.

"The beautiful marble building itself is a model
one. In the basement are located the game rooms, with
two pool tables, and other games; two regulation bowl-

ing alleys; the locker room; the marble toilet and bath rooms, equipped with shower, needle, sponge and tub baths. On the ground floor are the two reading rooms, supplied with 70 magazines and newspapers, a good number being in foreign languages; a pleasant parlor; well supplied writing tables; a convenient office for the general secretary; the fully equipped gymnasium 50 x 30 feet. On the first floor are three class rooms and the kitchen, while on the top floor there are four dormitories and a bath room.

"The educational work in Proctor has been, from its very beginning, a strong feature. In fact, this was one of the first Associations in the country to begin educational work for foreign-born men, and three months after the building was opened there was a class of 40 Hungarians studying English. From that time to the present year has seen large and interested groups in the various classes conducted. This year it has been necessary to use two of the dormitories in addition to the three regular class rooms for the work. The average enrolment in the classes was 61, and 47 of the men attended at least one-third of the class sessions, the total attendance being 1,115. There were five classes carried on, each meeting two nights each week for 20 weeks, and 17 Certificates of Merit were awarded to the men who attained a grade of 75 per cent for the work done and attendance. The five classes were: two in elementary English, with two instructors, enrolment 19, total attendance 518; one in advanced English, enrolment 6, total attendance 136; one in architectural and mechanical drawing, enrolment 15, total attendance 281; one in free-hand drawing and clay modeling, enrolment 7, total attendance 180. Most of the instructors have been college graduates, living in town.

"In one of the classes in Elementary English, however, the teacher, Charles Pulay, is a Hungarian. In November, 1909, he arrived at Proctor, not knowing a word of English. He entered a class at once, and has made such progress that this year he volunteered to teach this group of his fellow countrymen. A short time ago he and another man brought to General Secretary Mahaffy 25 applications for membership in this Association, from other Hungarians, each accompanied by the cash.

"The physical work this year, under the direction of Marcus Ling, a local Swedish man, has been the most successful for some years. Two classes each for seniors and juniors, have been held weekly, with good attendance. Beside the regular class work there have been basket ball and indoor baseball leagues, volley ball, and other games.

"The physical department raised the money to keep Beaver Pond cleared for skating all winter, and electric lights were strung around it. The department arranged two ice carnivals for the people of the whole village. The first was held on Christmas Day, with an attendance of over 500 people. The Proctor brass band played and refreshments were served. The second one was planned for Washington's Birthday, but had to be postponed because of the weather, and was held on the evening of Feb. 24. It was a masquerade affair, and there were many fine costumes, and prizes were given for the best woman's, man's, and couple's costumes. The evening was opened with a grand march on skates, followed by skating. The pond was strung with electric lights, there were fireworks, refreshments, and the Proctor band furnished music.

"The social atmosphere of the Association is always

warm and cordial, and beside the regular programme of general social work, special social affairs have been carried out by the four departments. One special event was the public reception given to the new superintendent of education, high school principal, and other school teachers.

"Another good piece of community service was the installation of moving picture entertainments in the village hall by the Association, which has proven to be one of the best things undertaken. About a year ago a first class machine was purchased and entertainments have been given Saturday nights since then. The larger part of the pictures have been of an educational character and they have furnished good, clean entertainment for the people, who have attended in large numbers.

"Beside the regular paid entertainments, several free ones have been given. One was on election night, when pictures were shown, returns received over two special wires, music furnished by the Proctor band. About 800 people attended, and the hall was packed until midnight. Another free entertainment was given to about 1,000 people one night in the summer on the park in connection with the weekly band concert.

"The Association also has maintained for a number of years a course of high class lectures and entertainments.

"In March, 1911, a troop of boy scouts was organized, when 18 boys were enrolled. The work has been a great help to the members, and has been the means of some splendid changes in the lives of some of the boys. Five nationalities are represented by the 20 members, and the first two boys in Vermont to become first class scouts are members of this troop, as is one life saver."

CAVENDISH HOUSE

ORMSBEE HOUSE

In later years, the men have been given a taste of this kind of life, through membership in the Green Mountain Club, the Proctor division of which was fathered by M. R. Proctor.

"It surely is true that the Proctor Association has been equal to the expectations for it, and from its beginning to the present time has been serving men of all classes, creeds, nationalities, in the spirit of true brotherhood."

And now for the postscript. In 1919 it was brought out in conference that while the organization had made a thoroughly efficient record under the title of Y. M. C. A., it could do still more under a broader code. From the beginning its purpose had been to serve the largest number of the town's young men. It was started and partially supported by the Company, that employees of all creeds and beliefs might get together in a social way under conditions altogether wholesome and democratic. It was agreed, therefore, that the entrance way should be made still broader in an effort to enroll all worthy candidates in unrestricted membership. That is how it came about that the old name was discarded May 1, 1919, when the sign of "Sutherland Club" appeared above the door.

The secretary of the Y. M. C. A., Mr. Mahaffy, is now the secretary of the Sutherland Club. As under the old regime the policy of the institution is formulated by a board of directors, although not a little of the responsibility is turned over to the membership committees. All in all, the gray rock-faced building on the square was never so thoroughly in sympathy with its peculiar mission. Strengthened by experience it can but be more adept in attacking the larger problems of the future.

* * * * * * * *

All this has to do with the boy's future. How about the girls? Their interests are being studied and served at Cavendish House, another of those social welfare projects which have grown up within the town.

"The work which Cavendish House now does began in January, 1910, in two rooms in the Post Office building, with one teacher who gave cooking lessons to adults and school children. The purpose originally was to teach these pupils to get better meals for less money, through a knowledge of the most approved methods of cooking inexpensive foods.

"In a few weeks an assistant was needed and the next autumn sewing was taught in addition to cooking, and English lessons, whenever they were needed, were given to foreign women.

"In 1913, as the work had outgrown its quarters, a small tenement house about half the size of the present building, was erected, and in 1917, it was increased to its present accommodations.

"The work from year to year has varied considerably to meet the need of any special time. During the war a woman came from Boston to teach surgical dressings, and a great number of these were made and sent to the Red Cross, as well as sheets and towels for hospitals, bath robes, etc. Gardening was taught for a few seasons and a summer school has sometimes been held at Cavendish House for pupils who did not pass in the public school, but who were anxious to make up their work before the fall term opened. During the influenza epidemic, cooking was done at Cavendish House to help out sick families.

"The following courses have been taught at various times: cooking, sewing, knitting, English (to foreign women), surgical dressings (during the war), physics, household accounting, history and geography of foods, hygiene, millinery, basketry, typewriting (summer, 1914), physical culture.

"At the present time a regular course is given in connection with the public school, in home making, which includes various subjects listed above.

"Bath and shampoo rooms are free to all women and children who wish to use them.

"A school nurse follows up absences from school and watches out for contagious diseases, bad teeth, diseased tonsils, defective eyes, and suggests special feeding for children who are underweight.

"For several years past, a club for young women has been organized, known as 'Cavendish Club,' which meets Thursday evenings, when courses in various subjects have been given, varied by social gatherings on special evenings during the month.

"This past winter Monday evenings have been given over to meetings for Polish and Finnish women; Tuesday evenings for Hungarian women and Slavs. These meetings have been chiefly for social times, but opportunity was given to any of these women to be instructed in sewing or cooking, if they so desired.

"For the children who come from farms quite a distance out of town, hot lunches have been served at Cavendish House at a minimum cost; also, this year, milk has been served to school children at a slight charge."

* * * * * * * *

It was in 1899 that the Proctor Hospital issued its first printed report. The building in which it was housed has since been made over into the Proctor Inn. The original owner was F. P. Bartlett. He had started it as a home for himself but had died before it was

PROCTOR HOSPITAL, 1896 TO 1902

THE HOSPITAL

ready for his occupancy. It then took its place among the Company's houses. The last tenant was J. C. Cameron.

This first hospital, which was in reality a welfare project instituted by the Vermont Marble Company, was declared ready for service in August, 1896. It was the direct outgrowth of a resultful experiment of the previous year whereby trained nurses were employed at Proctor and West Rutland to care for those who were ill among the employees and their families. The hospital staff was to join hands with the district nurses, and together they were to administer to a larger clientele.

Reading through the brief synopsis in that report of 1899 we can but feel a growing respect for what appears in retrospect like a little cottage with a big name. Observe the air of completeness and repressed pride in this descriptive paragraph:

"The plans were drawn after a careful inspection of some of the best of the smaller modern hospitals. The building is heated by a combination hot air and hot water furnace, and each room is ventilated by a separate flue running to the roof. Hot and cold water are distributed at convenient points throughout the building. The plumbing and drainage have been examined and approved by the best sanitary experts. The housekeeping rooms are on the second floor. The accident and operating rooms are fully equipped with modern tables and instruments, and the whole hospital is provided with all modern appliances and conveniences. An ambulance has been recently added to the equipment. Ten patients can be conveniently accommodated, and, in case of emergency, a larger number."

Then follows a plea for cooperation coupled with a word or two regarding matters of policy:

'The hospital is intended primarily for the benefit of the Company's employees and their families, but others, and especially residents of the communities where the different branches of its business are located, will be admitted as pay patients. It is the Company's desire that the people of these communities should be interested as generally as possible in the conduct and success of the hospital. Its management has accordingly been committed to a representative board, in accordance with the annexed by-laws, and the Company especially urges that this entire board take an active interest and part in its management. The limited income received from the board of pay patients is used toward the expenses of the hospital. Beyond that, it is the purpose of the Vermont Marble Company to furnish the management, from time to time, with such sums of money, as it may need to properly conduct the hospital in keeping with the plan contemplated in its foundation."

In the year book of 1911, this paragraph appears:

"The rapid growth of the work and the satisfactory results obtained from the outset rendered it necessary to provide a larger and more modern building. Consequently the present building was built and equipped by the Company and was opened for the admission of patients April 1, 1904. It is located on Ormsbee Avenue in the eastern part of the Village of Proctor, faces south and west, and commands a fine view of the surrounding country.

"The operating room, accident room, surgeons' consulting room, and etherizing room, and the matron's office and the nurses' living rooms are in the Adminis-

tration Building. This is built of rock-faced marble
with partitions of fireproof tile, plastered upon wire
lath, and is throughout of fireproof construction. The
entire hospital and its equipment, and especially the
operating room, is thoroughly up-to-date and em-
bodies the latest approved devices in use in the newest
hospitals in our large cities. It accommodates eighteen
patients."

Again, in a publication of 1916, there is the record
of further growth.

"In 1904 the present hospital building was erected
with a capacity of eighteen patients. In 1913 improvements were made, increasing the capacity to thirty
patients. The changes consisted of an obstetrical ward
an obstetrical case room, additional quarters for the
nurses, improved and enlarged kitchen facilities and a
solarium.

"The work of the hospital has been much extended
during the past few years. The total number of house
patients received for treatment during 1915 was 327,
which is the largest number in the history of the hospital. The total number of outside patients during the
year was 506, a total number of patients for the year
of 833. The total number of house patients from 1911
to 1915 inclusive, was 1,384 and the total number of
outside patients for the same period was 2,734.

"The high standard of efficiency in training the
student nurses has been maintained and the graduates
of this training school are highly regarded by the medi-
ical profession."

Since these lines were written it has seemed best
to discontinue for the time at least the training school
for nurses.

                *   *   *   *   *   *   *

"Ormsbee House is a school and home for crippled children. It was opened the first of January, 1921, admitting both boys and girls between the ages of six and twelve, and has a capacity for fifteen. It was expected to take only those children who had been crippled as a result of infantile paralysis, and so far but one other case has been taken.

"No payment towards the ordinary care and maintenance of the children is required, though parents may contribute anything toward the work that they like and are expected to provide clothing and to take care of expenses other than those incurred in connection with the boarding and schooling of the children; as, for example, dentistry and special medical treatment or care because of other illness.

"Children are given carefully regulated and prescribed exercises daily and their school work is arranged according to their strength and capacity, with the idea of putting them forward in the ordinary grade work as rapidly as possible. No children below full normal mentality are admitted but, of course, most of them, because of their infirmity, have been kept out of school so much that they are behind the normal grade for their age.

"Children are selected because of their inability, owing to their infirmity, to attend school at home or any public school; because of the financial needs of their parents and their particular need of care and special exercises to assist in the improvement of their disability and upbuilding of their general health.

"The institution is open all the year around, the children continuing in school throughout the year except for a two or three-weeks vacation in the summer. The children are selected and sent to the school largely by the infantile paralysis after-care workers in the state."

CHAPTER X

A REVIEW OF THE SCRAP BOOKS

PRESIDENTIAL VISITS AND OTHER IMPORTANT
GATHERINGS—THE COMMUNITY IDEA—
PROCTOR IN THE WORLD WAR—
CONCLUSION

IN the vaults at the Company's office are three venerable scrap-books. They are made up of newspaper clippings and printed matter of varied kinds, and every paragraph preserved therein relates in some way to the town or its industry. Indeed these books are in themselves a history, although like all such collections they use many pages in covering the ground.

The only way they could be drafted into the service of this final chapter was by cutting out little sections here and there, lines which treat of happenings not previously reviewed. If then the composition that follows seems almost too much like patchwork, the reader will understand that it suffers from being transplanted from the scrap-books.

A circular dated March 30, 1887, announces the adoption by the Vermont Marble Company of an accident insurance plan which was to apply to all employees. On the back of that same page, was the notice of a Savings Department, established Dec. 1, 1888, whereby the workers could deposit their money with the Company, under banking regulations. This latter experiment was the corner-stone of the Proctor Trust Company, which was organized in 1891.

A little farther along in the book is a small handbill reading as follows:

"Everybody invited to welcome President Harrison, Friday evening, August 28, 1891. The torch-light procession will form north of Vermont Marble Company's office at 7:30 o'clock. Reception at Governor Redfield Proctor's grounds at 8:30. Everyone asked to illuminate their residences and make the town as attractive as possible. Let us give him a genuine Vermont welcome."

Then follows the newspaper story of the celebration. Only a small part of it can be quoted—just enough to illustrate how well Proctor responded to the appeal.

"Early in the evening the houses of Secretary Proctor (Secretary of War in Harrison's Cabinet) and the offices of the Company were lighted up. Then colored lights began to show on the piazzas and to fringe the edges of the road. They came from Chinese lanterns hung at brief intervals. Before the full blackness of the night had come on, the little village was in colored lights, while from an arch in front of Secretary Proctor's house the word 'WELCOME' gleamed in letters of fire. At 8 o'clock a procession started from the Company's store. It was headed by the Proctor band. The line of march was through the village whose streets wind around the side of the hills in which Proctor is built. The village people to the number of nearly a thousand had gathered on the lawn of Mr. Proctor's house and in the roadway before it. As the torchlight procession approached the Proctor mansion a great flame leaped up from the top of the mountain across the valley, more than a mile away. Answering it, signal fires flamed from a dozen hilltops all around, while through the village columns of fire from great torches of pitch and shavings made the cloud-hung heaven red with their glare. From the hills to the left also rockets and bombs were sent up. Across the valley was stretched half a mile of Chinese lanterns. It was five minutes of nine when the head of the procession reached Secretary Proctor's house."

Referring to the demonstration the President said at the outset of his Proctor speech: "This journey in Vermont is crowned tonight by a reception and a good-bye that is surprisingly brilliant and artistic in its preparation, and one that I have never seen excelled."

In the morning the village was again breathing naturally. Mr. Harrison had departed, and Proctor had entertained its first president.

Under date of Feb. 13, 1893, appears an account of the most serious quarry accident ever experienced by the Company. A scale of marble 65 feet long, 16 feet wide, with a maximum thickness of three feet, crashed down from the roof of a tunnel, giving no warning to the men who were working under it.

To quote from the newspaper story: "The worst disaster in the history of Vermont marble quarrying came Saturday afternoon, when a mass of stone fell from overhead in a West Rutland quarry and instantly killed five men and injured ten others. The accident was in the famous Sheldon covered quarry, operated by the Vermont Marble Company, near the extremity of work, downward and eastward over 500 feet from the surface of the ground. The mass of rock fell upon one gang of men only. The time was about 1:15 o'clock, soon after the men had returned to work."

Following this picture of the quarry horror, are

SENATOR PROCTOR'S RESIDENCE AT TIME OF PRESIDENT McKINLEY'S VISIT several newspaper columns devoted to McKinley's first visit to Vermont. That was in August, 1892, when he was governor of Ohio. He simply called at Proctor on that initial trip, but in August, 1897, he came again and stayed over night at the home of Senator Proctor, thus giving the town a chance to welcome another president.

The local paper had this to say of the occasion: "United States Senator Proctor's residence last night was the scene of a remarkable popular demonstration. Over a thousand people congregated to welcome the President and his friends. All Proctor and the children were there; four hundred of Rutland's citizens were there; the Proctor Brass Band was there. The eye and ear and the imagination had enough to feed on last night. About the Senator's house is a formidable barricade of shrubbery. Last night some artist had hung in this choice vegetation a profusion of incandescent lights—red, white and blue. Dark hedges were transformed into intricate brackets for brilliant color effects. Handsome trees were articulated in electric rays. A fountain had no end of sport playing with nearly every color of the rainbow. The American flag, attached to a pole surmounted by a circle of electric lights, posed in patriotic attitude in the still night air, and every arch, cornice and line of the house was so accentuated by electricity that the moon over-head seemed to shed a dim apology for living."

The President was accompanied by Mrs. McKinley and by his Secretary of War, General Alger. Vice-President and Mrs. Hobart were also members of the party, but they were the guests of friends in Rutland.

It could not be foreseen then that five years later the people of the marble town would again be assembled

on Senator Proctor's grounds in honor of another
president. But such was the fortune of the years. A
handbill in letters of red looks out at us from the scrap
book pages. It is worded, in part, as follows:

"PRESIDENT ROOSEVELT AT PROCTOR, SEPT. 1, 1902.

"President Roosevelt and party will arrive at
Proctor at 11:50 A. M., and remain until 12:20 P. M.
He will speak to the people from the piazza of Senator
Proctor's house. The Proctor Band will give a concert
on the lawn before the arrival of the presidential party.
A special train for Rutland will leave Proctor at 12:30,
immediately after the departure of the President."

On the same page with the handbill is a clipping
from the New York Commercial, half of which is given
up to a report of Mr. Roosevelt's speech, and the remainder to a playful recital of the efforts of the village
to "slick up" for the celebration. It was averred that
one end of the covered bridge—the only end the President was to see—was given a whitewash bath; that the
railway station was painted for the first time since its
roof was raised, with freshly washed windows bidding
further defiance to a fixed policy; also that a special
hemlock hedge was imported over night to hide an
ugly fence along the line of parade. Yet all these little
gibes could detract little from the renown that the village had earned as an entertainer of presidents.

In June, 1903, came the reunion of the 15th Vermont Regiment, when Colonel Proctor had as guests
on his 73rd birthday his "boys of sixty-one." The
special train provided by the host, which started at
Newport and wound around through Barton, Lyndon-
ville, Wells River, St. Johnsbury and Montpelier, had
collected about 250 passengers by the time it reached

Proctor. Of this reception by the Senator and his helpers—the lunch in the Y. M. C. A., the sight-seeing in and around Proctor, the band concert and the speeches—the newspapers were most appreciative and many were the fine things they said about the town and its founder. They also took up in detail the events of the evening in Rutland, with the dinner at the Berwick and the campfire in G. A. R. Hall, and the trip of the next forenoon to the West Rutland quarries, even the baskets of lunch which were brought into the train at Proctor when the "special" was setting out on its homeward trail.

"The only surprise of the day for Senator Proctor," declared one of the papers, "and the only thing in the arrangement of which he had no part, was when he was presented with a very handsome gold-headed cane by his regimental comrades. It was cleverly presented by Adj. J. T. Gleason in a well-worded speech in which the love and esteem with which the Colonel was held by his men was briefly but eloquently portrayed."

Another paper observed that "the handsome new free hospital just opened was of great interest to the visitors, but the mecca for the veterans was the grave of 'Old Charley,' Senator Proctor's war horse that served him so faithfully. The horse was purchased originally in Lyndon and was a Morgan of the most pronounced type. His grave is marked by a twenty-ton block of marble."

Down in one corner of the page, almost out of sight, is a printed copy of the resolutions adopted at one of the later meetings of the regiment, lines which radiate appreciation and the spirit of true comradeship. Notice how they still regarded themselves as the Colonel's "boys":

REUNION OF 15TH VERMONT REGIMENT, 1904

"Whereas, we the survivors of the 15th Reg't Vt. Vols., to the number of one hundred and fifty-two members, have been by invitation the guests of Redfield Proctor, our Colonel in the late Civil War, in an excursion by special train from Newport to Proctor and return.

"Resolved, that we, together with our wives and daughters, also invited members of the party, express our sincere thanks for the royal hospitality everywhere and in every conceivable way shown us.

"Resolved, that upon this the seventy-third anniversary of his birth, we tender him the full meed of our admiration, esteem and goodwill, with the hope that his present vigor may continue for many years more, to bless us, his boys, his native state, his country and the world at large."

The year 1904 was marked by a concerted attempt on the part of the labor agitators to create dissension in the ranks of the marble workers. Older residents will remember the days of the strike, an ordeal which began with great acclamation, spun itself out through several weeks, and finally settled down into an abject failure. It was an effort to do away with the piece-work basis and unionize the shops. The one obstacle which could not well be displaced was that the shops as a whole had no desire for a change.

While this strike was in progress, the Company sent a general letter to all its customers. This is being reproduced almost in its entirety, not alone because it applies forcefully to that particular crisis, but because it is an able summary of the labor policy, which has grown up with the industry.

"A strike was begun here last month involving a small number of our employees. It was instigated and is being managed by parties from New York and Chicago. These outside managers have sent out distorted and wilfully false reports concerning the strike itself and generally concerning our business and employees. As these reports have been published broadcast, very likely they may have come to your attention. We have refused to be drawn into any newspaper discussion of the matter, but in justice to our relations with you we now take this way to give you briefly the facts.

"We employ in Vermont about 2,500 men—the number in June was 2,474. We employ both union and non-union men. The exact proportion of each the first of July we do not know, but probably four-fifths of the whole were not members of any union. There was no complaint from our employees, either union or non-union, against the general conditions and scale of wages prevailing here, and our relations were mutually satisfactory.

"Such being the situation, some time in June a stranger from New York city called upon us and demanded that we 'unionize' our entire business and agree in writing that we would not employ any but union men. Of course we refused. A strike was ordered, and on July 12th some of our union employees, obeying the order, went out. A week later these outside parties attempted to force out all of our employees, but only a few of them paid any attention to this latter order. The largest number of our men who have been out at any time is 225, or about seven per cent of the whole. Ninety-three per cent of our employees, including union men, have remained loyal to us in spite of all outside interference and misrepresentations. Some of those who went out have gone back to work. There are now

MARBLE CROWNED GRAVE OF OLD CHARLEY, SENATOR PROCTOR'S
ARMY HORSE

about 175 who have not returned, of whom a part have
gone away to seek work elsewhere and the rest are remaining quietly here. Our relations with them continue entirely amicable. All of them who were renting
houses of the Company are still occupying them with our
full consent, including the families of those who have
gone away to seek work elsewhere. They have talked
freely with our different officers and superintendents,
and they make no complaint of the general conditions
or scale of wages existing here, but say that they went
out because they were ordered out, and stay out because they dare not return.

"About 110 of them are Italian stone cutters.
Apart from them the strike would not have affected
us at all. As a whole they were good men and good
workmen, and they were earning good wages. For

example, in one shop there were many who earned over $4 per day, and the average of the whole forty-six who went out of that shop, including several apprentices and a number who could not do a full day's work, was over $3 per day. To them it is represented that whether they stay out or go back we shall be compelled to unionize our business; that if they disobey the orders of the union now they will be blacklisted and soon will not be permitted to work at their trade as stone cutters, either for us or any one else. This threat, coupled also with the fear of being blacklisted in Italy, has been sufficient to restrain the great bulk of them from returning to their work, although many of them freely express their desire to do so.

"It is the claim of these outside manipulators that the men who went out were compelled to strike because they were only paid starvation wages, and that their wages were all taken by the Company for rent and store accounts. The average rent of our houses occupied by the men who went out was $5.07 per month. The tyranny of the Company's stores has been especially dwelt upon. It amounts to simply this: Neither the Vermont Marble Company nor its managers and owners have one cent of interest in the profits of its stores. They are run on a co-operative basis, solely for the convenience and profit of the employees themselves. Their prices are reasonable and their outside sales to customers, in no way connected with the Company, amount to over one hundred thousand dollars per year. At the end of the year the business of each store is settled under the supervision of a committee of the employees. In that settlement the company is allowed four per cent interest on the money it advances for the conduct of the store business, and also receives

nothing either for general superintendence or otherwise, but the entire profits of the sales both to employees and to non-employees are then divided among
the trading employees in proportion to their trade.
At the end of last year there was paid back to the trading employees in cash at our Proctor store 10 per cent
on the amount of their purchases; at our West Rutland
store 9 per cent, and at our Center Rutland store 6
per cent. This Company has not one cent of interest
in whether its employees trade at its store or not and is
absolutely indifferent thereto. Instead of the men's
wages being eaten up by their rent and store accounts,
the fact is that during the year ending June 30th last,
less than 3 per cent of the entire wages of all our employees was retained by the Company for rent, less
than 22 per cent of it went to these cooperative stores,
and over 75 per cent was paid in actual cash to our
employees.

"As to the general conditions of employment and
scale of wages of our employees, they are satisfactory
enough to our men themselves to have attracted to us
as good and as faithful a set of men as can be found
anywhere. On the average our skilled employees have
been with us for many years, and to say that they are
not able or independent enough to leave if they want to
is a greater slander of them than of us. There are some
necesary differences between employment in the country and in the city. A good many of our men own their
own homes, but being in a rural community apart from
any large center of population we are compelled to furnish houses for many. The cost of rent and of store
goods has already been mentioned. Other expenses
also are relatively smaller in the country. For example,
the best of milk is sold in the village of Proctor the

THE INN

FORESTER'S HALL

year around at four cents per quart, and coal is delivered
from 50c to 75c per ton less than it can be purchased
in the neighboring city of Rutland. This is not the time
or place to discuss our efforts in behalf of the welfare
of our men, but we may mention two things which bear
directly upon their opportunity to save. We carry entirely at our own expense and without the action or cooperation of our employees in any way a general accident policy which covers all of our employees from the
moment they enter our employ. Under this policy in
case of accident our men receive free medical attendance
and one-half wages while they are laid up, or in case of
death, their family receives $500. We also maintain
at our own expense a free hospital where our employees
and their families receive free treatment and from
which, without expense, in case of sickness at their
homes, they are furnished the services of a nurse. These
and other similiar provisions for our employees are not
in substitution for their wages or any part of them, but
simply additional to them. It is a sufficient comment
upon the slander that our employees are poverty-
stricken, that in the village of Proctor with less than
2500 inhabitants, a village built up entirely upon the
business of this Company and consisting almost wholly
of its employees and their families, there are over 700
persons who have deposits in one savings bank besides
their deposits in other institutions.

"Knowing the general desire of the strikers to return to work, we waited patiently several weeks to give
them an opportuntiy. Only recently have we begun
to fill their places. There has been no shortage whatever
in the quarries or mills. Our only inconvenience has
been in the cutting department of our finishing shops.

"The attempt to boycott our marble has been a

failure. Our monumental business has been absolutely untouched by it. In our building marble business our marble is being handled and set satisfactorily everywhere. Every job which we have the contract to set is being set regularly; and the same is true of every job where our marble was contracted to be set by others, except only one job which is at present tied up for reasons entirely independent of us or the situation here. In only one city has there been any serious interruption, and the entire limit of such interruption only amounted to a few days. There are thirty-six setters now setting our marble in that city."

As a relief from the pages of labor discussion, there is inserted a section from the Burlington Free Press of August 4, 1905, which reports the mid-summer outing of the Vermont Association of Boston.

"About eleven o'clock this morning (August 3rd) the party boarded special trolley cars at Rutland, provided through the courtesy of the Hon. Fletcher D. Proctor, and proceeded to Center Rutland where they were joined by Gov. C. J. Bell, Collector of Customs, Olin Merrill, Mr. Merrill of the firm of Merrill, Oldham and Co., Boston, Frank L. Greene of the St. Albans Messenger, J. L. Southwich of the Burlington Free Press.

"President Proctor of the Vermont Marble Company together with Col. E. R. Morse, the Hon. Frank C. Partridge, who had just returned the day before from a European trip, Superintendents Taylor and Higbee and other officials of the Company, were at the recreation house of the Company in Center Rutland where the guests were welcomed. The finishing shops and mills at that point were visited and twelve office employes, detailed for the purpose, explained to the visitors every process employed in putting the rough stone in readiness for the market.

"The party then boarded a special train over the Clarendon & Pittsford railroad and proceeded to West Rutland where the most famous marble quarries on the continent were visited.

"After visiting the Company's club house at West Rutland the party proceeded by special train to Proctor where they were escorted to the Y. M. C. A. building. The guests were welcomed by the host and by Mrs. Fletcher D. Proctor, Miss Proctor and Redfield Proctor, Jr., who were assisted in dispensing hospitality by the young people of the place. An appetizing as well as an elaborate luncheon was served in the gymnasium, which had been transformed for the time being into a beautifully decorated banquet hall. While the different courses were being served by the young ladies in a manner that would have done credit to the best hotel in the land, the Proctor Cornet Band of twenty-four pieces, which is concedeed to be one of the finest in the state, discoursed its choicest music, interspersed with excellent solos and choruses by a choir of young ladies.

"After the banquet, the party assembled on the spacious marble steps leading to the building and had its picture taken. This was followed by an inspection of the works in Proctor. Not the least interesting object seen there was the new power plant with its immense penstock nine feet in diameter, which will develop over 3,000 horse power."

It may have been noticed that in all these big days of Proctor the band has been one of the contributing factors, thus qualifying itself to stand as one of the abiding institutions of the town. Nor is its claim to

VIEW OF THE FLOOD, 1913—LOOKING SOUTH FROM BRIDGE

permanency based on scrap-book history alone. One of the stories which was passed along to Harry Powers by Morris Reynolds relates to the Sutherland Falls Brass Band, organized back in the thirties, a company of musicians whose accomplishments were well advertised throughout this section of the country. Their greatest conquest took place in Montreal, where they went to play for the celebration which marked the crowning of Queen Victoria. Morris Reynolds was a member of this band; the Humphrey brothers also were numbered among its active supporters. Some of the instruments then in service are still being kept by the descendants of those pioneer band men.

Going back again to the scrap book, the next item to call a halt is one under date of April 9, 1907, headed "Weekly Payments" with a sub-title which declares that the "Vermont Marble Company has completed details for paying out over $26,000 every week". After explaining the new addressograph method of making out the vouchers and envelopes, it goes on to say that "with the inauguration of the weekly payment system the Company stores at Proctor, West Rutland and Center Rutland will be placed on a strictly cash basis, but with the continuance of the cooperative benefits. In place of credit books, the men will be asked to purchase coupon books."

Two days of July, 1908, were set apart for the reception of the Vermont Press Association. The guests first assembled at Pittsford for an inspection of the new Vermont Sanitorium. Covering this phase of the trip the Waterbury Record observes that "all were unanimous in saying that the late Hon. Redfield Proctor had given to Vermont an institution which could always stand as a lasting memorial of a great man, one whom

VIEW OF THE FLOOD, 1913—ENTRANCE TO COOPERATIVE STORE

VIEW OF THE FLOOD, 1913—REAR OF PROCTOR STATION

Vermont had seen fit to honor and one who in turn had honored Vermont."

On another page of the book are several more columns relating to the sanitorium, the story leading up to its completion and the officials into whose hands it was committed. This however, is too recent for emphasis, nor would it be altogether in keeping with the present, for the entire property has since been turned over to the State.

From Pittsford the newspaper men went by train to Rutland, where the feature of the evening was a banquet at the Bardwell Hotel. On the second day, continuing as guests of Governor Proctor, the visitors were taken to the West Rutland quarries and later to Proctor where they were given the usual freedom of the shops and mills with a luncheon in the gymnasium.

This completes the review of the scrap-books. And is it not time well spent to go over these motley leaves of the past and pick out the most alluring headlines? Aside from all thought of the incident involved, there is no other way equally forceful of portraying and analyzing the community spirit which first became assertive in the days of old Sutherland Falls.

This spirit had its beginning in gatherings of which there is no record save in the memories of some of those who were there. The twenty-first birthday of Fletcher D. Proctor was given wide acclaim by a supper and dance. The only hall then available for a party of such magnitude was the expansive store room over Patterson's Mill, and there it was that the neighbors assembled to present their best wishes to the one who was then starting on the road to leadership. James Haney was one of the floor directors of the evening.

Another big day of still more remote times, was

VIEW OF THE FLOOD, 1913—NEAR HUMPHREY'S SIDING

the one which commemorated the election of Col.
Redfield Proctor as governor of Vermont. Then, as in
the case of the presidential visits, the grounds of the
Proctor home were transformed into an outdoor reception room.

Sometime in the long ago too there was a day
when all the school children were brought together in
the old Coping Shop. The plan and purpose of the
jubilee have long since been forgotten. Memory simply
insists that it took place and goes no further.

Looking the other way from the scrap-book period
—the way which leads down to present day activities—
there is almost no limit to the historical data which is
entitled to recognition. This little book, however, can
never hope to be considered complete. It aims rather to
keep itself small and bind together only the big elements of the story. Ignoring, therefore, the blizzard

of March, 1888, when the Rutland train had to be shoveled out of the cut beside the Building Shop, and the flood of 1913, when water from the river flowed through the railway cut south of the station, it is better far to hurry along and leave many of the later events to be filled in by the reader.

It is inevitable that this allusion to the flood should bring in another paragraph on the marble bridge which was erected in 1915 by Mrs. Emily J. Proctor, as a memorial to her son, Gov. Fletcher D. Proctor. There is something perennially inspiring about this pile of marble. As a thing of beauty, as a bulwark against the floods and ice-jams of the future, as a symbol of the permanency of the town and its institutions, speaking always of a purposeful life, it stands far removed from the multitude of commonplace memorials.

Another landmark which will be likely to gain richer, deeper meaning with the passing years is the Old Library Building or Municipal Memorial. It is destined to become the storehouse for a world of cherished memories and as such it will be dedicated anew by the generations that are yet unborn.

The World War is too recent a thing for appraisal or discussion. What it was and how it came to Proctor is well known to every reader of today. As a reminder for the reader of tomorrow, however, that they may not be unmindful of the sacrifices of the community, it is essential that this brief service roll be inserted. It is taken from the bound volume of War Echoes—circulars which went out from the Company's office bearing items of interest to the men in the camps.

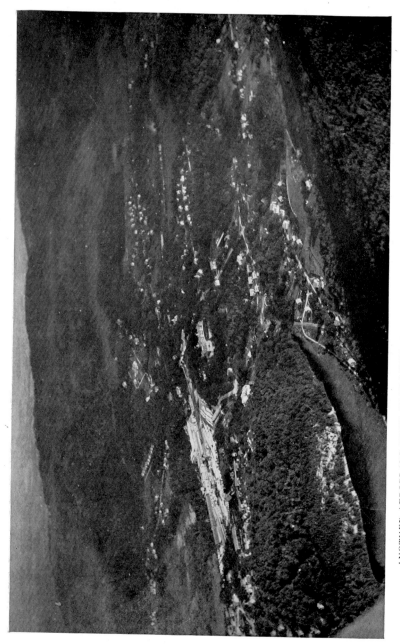

ANOTHER AEROPLANE VIEW OF PROCTOR, TAKEN AT A HIGHER ALTITUDE AND SHOWING MORE OF THE SURROUNDING COUNTRY

ROLL OF HONOR

ARMY

Allard, Andrew
Allen, S. T.
Anderson, H. E.
Anderson, Birger
Anoe, Raymond
Baird, Leslie, West Rutland
Baldwin, Leon
Baratta, Frank
Barommo, John, Middlebury
Battles, Barney, West Rutland
Belfonte, Pacifico, Florence
Bengston, C. H., St. Louis
Benoir, Charles
Binder, Edw. F.
Blakey, Harley J., West Rutland
Brown, Russell, Florence
Brown, Abel, Florence
Brown, Harry, West Rutland
Cain, Wm., West Rutland
Calozezo, Lipura, West Rutland
Carlson, August, West Rutland
Carrigan, John E.
Coffin, Holland, Cleveland
Congo, F. E., Cleveland
Charnecky, Joseph (Reservist)
Costa, Virginia, Center Rutland
Daly, A. J., Florence
Demsey, John, West Rutland
Dickenson, Frank, Roxbury
Donnelly, Henry J.
Drake, F. J., Florence
Dromey, J. M., Cleveland
Ducette, Jerome, Florence
Durillo, Alesandro
Eni, Tony, (Died at Camp Devens)
Erickson, Edward
Erickson, Peter
Faley, Frank E.
Fleming, John P., Center Rutland
Frappier, Victor
Garrow, Frank E.
Gatti, Egisto, Florence
Gault, Wm., West Rutland

Geno, George, Jr.
Gilbert, Ovila
Goss, Ernest, Middlebury
Gustafson, Carl W.
Gustafson, Herman
Haase, Richard
Hamilton, Wm. J., West Rutland
Haney, Chas. L.
Hobbs, Wilson, Middlebury
Howard, L. R., Middlebury
Johnson, A. P., Dallas
Johnson, Carl W.
Johnson, Bernard
Johnson, Edwin, St. Louis
Johnson, Einar, West Rutland
Johnson, Herbert
Johnson, Oscar A., West Rutland
Johnson, Waldemar H.
Kapusto, Tony, West Rutland
Karlson, Karl
Kellogg, L. S. Florence
La Francis, Rowell, West Rutland
Lapan, George, Florence
Larson, Charles
Larson, Helge
Larson, Anders
Leahey, George, Center Rutland
Ledin, George
Lee, Allan
Lesniewski, Paul, Center Rutland
Lee, Allan
Lesniewski, Paul, Center Rutland
Lumbra, A. A.
Malli, John, Middlebury
Mallie, John, Middlebury
McDermott, Thos. P., Center Rutland
McLaughlin, J., Florence
McNeil, Wm. H.
McShane, B. J., Chicago
Minkler, Wilbur
Moran, Harold, Florence
Nelson, Gunnar
Neun, George, Roxbury
Nichol, A. D.
Noyes, Walter B., West Rutland

Nyberg, Carl
Olsen, Fritz, West Rutland
Oncy, John, Roxbury
Oscarson, Algot
Parker, Leo, West Rutland
Plimpton, F. J., Boston
Plock, John, Tacoma
Pollard, J. R.
Proctor, Mortimer R.
Putnam, John J., West Rutland
Rabitor, Frank
Raksanyi, Charles
Ratti, E. H.
Ravenna, Emanuel, Center Rutland
Rudin, Alfred, Cleveland
Rudin, Oscar, Center Rutland
Rusmussen Knuie, West Rutland
Ryder, F. H. L.
Sabourin, Fred J., West Rutland
Sachelli, Garibaldi, Florence
Sedergren, A'got
Settergren, John, Florence
Shedd, Frank, West Rutland
Simonds, Walter, Middlebury
Sisco, Carroll W.
Sjostrom, Ernest, Florence
Smith, Kenneth O.
Solari, Guiseppe
Spear, George
Stall, Frank
Stevens, Percy, Florence
Stomper, John J., Center Rutland
Strand, Carl
Swing, W. L., Tacoma
Teneranni, Almo
Thibault, Clovis
Thomas, C. C.
Torrance, V. C., St. Louis
Vozniak, Steve, Philadelphia
Wallet, Bert
Walsac, Peter, Florence
Warner, Harry, Huntington Falls
Washburn, Geo. E.
Woods, Wilfred, West Rutland
Wos, John, West Rutland
Zambelli, Hercules

ENGINEERING CORPS

Duski, Joe, Center Rutland
Grieg, W. M., Philadelphia
Lytle, J. W., Tacoma
Parkmen, E. H., West Rutland
Peterson, N. C.
Proctor, Redfield
Pugh, William, Boston

ORDNANCE DEPARTMENT

Eggleston, Geo. H.
Peterson, J. A.

QUARTERMASTERS RESERVE

Aronson, Hilding
Aronson, Melcher
Higbee, Paul
Rudin, John
Saylor, L. D., San Francisco

SIGNAL CORPS RESERVE

Kelley, T. C., West Rutland
Olson, Sigfrid, Cleveland

AVIATION

Burditt, Rollin
Fay, Wallace
Hamilton, A., Middlebury
Lafferty, R. G., Cleveland
Lindberg, A. J., Center Rutland
Ravenna, Geno, Center Rutland

NAVY

Beauchman, Geo.
Beauchman, Lucien
Bergren, Harry, West Rutland
Bjork, Sigfred
Devosa, Steve, West Rutland
Drop, Walter, West Rutland
Ellis, Star, Middlebury
Gleason, Leslie, St. Louis
Johnson, Alfred
Kallen, John
Ladabouche, Frank

Moriglioni, Batisca, Center Rutland
Middleton, A. J., San Francisco
Nelson, Geo., St. Louis
Nelson, John, St. Louis
North, Jack, Florence
Pease, E. A.

Ross, Albert, West Rutland
Segar, Robert, West Rutland
Swanson, Carl
Thibault, A. F.
Thompson, C. A.

The foregoing is believed to be a complete list of the men who left the employment of the Vermont Marble Company to enter the nation's military service.

SUMMARY OF WAR WORK

'Population of Proctor, 1910, census, 2,871; Oct., 1918, estimates at 2,200; 24 nationalities. In service (from Proctor homes or working here when entering service) about 160. Of this number about 22 are commissioned officers and 45 non-commissioned officers.

In Red Cross and Y. M. C. A. work, 5.

Red Cross membership—Oct., 1918, 523; Jan., 1919, 839.

Red Cross State Supply Service located here for 4 months—distributing without expense to 155 Vermont Chapters supplies valued at $35,000.

Work of Proctor Branch—Red Cross to Aug. 1, 1919:

Sweaters	436	Mufflers	79
Socks	1076 prs.	Refugee garments (new)	599
Wristlets	277 prs.	Hospital articles	1369
Helmets	55	Surgical dressings	21,351

Front line packets (containing 7 dressings)   807

1st appeal Belgian Relief Nov. 1917— 835 lbs. used clothing
2nd appeal Belgian Relief Oct. 1918—1565 lbs. used clothing
3rd appeal Belgian Relief Apr. 1919— 720 lbs. used clothing

	Quota	Raised	Subscriptions	Per cent of Population
1st Liberty Loan		$265,750.00	431	15
2nd Liberty Loan	$207,000.00	407,500.00	481	17
3rd Liberty Loan	88,600.00	393,650.00	428	15
4th Liberty Loan	177,000.00	492,700.00	676	23½
5th Liberty Loan	144,000.00	649,400.00	594	21
1st Red Cross Drive				$28,310.00
2nd Red Cross Drive				10,252.00
Gifts and entertainments for Red Cross				1,021.00
Knights of Columbus				1,250.00
Y. M. C. A.				6,550.00
War Library Fund (quota $150.00)				300.00
United War Work Drive (quota $10,600)				12,900.00

Books for Camp Libraries, 648 copies

War Savings—First town in County—with per capita sales
    (Maturity value on Sept. 14, 1918)   16.50

Per capita pledged in June drive based on 1910 census   22.50

After scanning these figures and taking reverent measure of Proctor's participation in the Great Con- flict, it seems almost like sacrilege to come down again to the drab background of the present. And after all why should anyone wish to prolong the narrative. True, the big field of today is left almost untouched, but even the far corners of today are within everyone's knowledge. It is quite logical, therefore, to bring the story up to the later years and then cut it off without ceremony.

With this one paragraph then, which is reprinted through the courtesy of Personal Efficiency, the curtain falls and the type trails off into white space.

"By this means Proctor has been moulded into something more than a mere collection of houses. Not alone are the residents surrounded by modern con- veniences; they are offered every incentive to growth and advancement. No man need feel that his ability is likely to be underrated or that his house and children are in danger of contamination. The growth of the Vermont Marble industry holds a real lesson for in- dustrial ventures of all kinds. It represents the life work of a man who believed in American marble and who succeeded, not only in giving stability to the in- dustry but in bequeathing to his workmen something more than a chance to earn their bread."